Editor-in-Chief and Founder:
  Lyndon H. LaRouche, Jr.
Editorial Board: *Lyndon H. LaRouche, Jr. , Helga Zepp-LaRouche, Paul Gallagher, Tony Papert, Gerald Rose, Dennis Small, Jeffrey Steinberg, William Wertz*
Co-Editors: *Paul Gallagher, Tony Papert*
Managing Editor: *Nancy Spannaus*
Technology: *Marsha Freeman*
Books: *Katherine Notley*
Ebooks: *Richard Burden*
Graphics: *Alan Yue*
Photos: *Stuart Lewis*
Circulation Manager: *Stanley Ezrol*

INTELLIGENCE DIRECTORS
Counterintelligence: *Jeffrey Steinberg, Michele Steinberg*
Economics: *John Hoefle, Marcia Merry Baker, Paul Gallagher*
History: *Anton Chaitkin*
Ibero-America: *Dennis Small*
Russia and Eastern Europe: *Rachel Douglas*
United States: *Debra Freeman*

INTERNATIONAL BUREAUS
Bogotá: *Miriam Redondo*
Berlin: *Rainer Apel*
Copenhagen: *Tom Gillesberg*
Houston: *Harley Schlanger*
Lima: *Sara Madueño*
Melbourne: *Robert Barwick*
Mexico City: *Gerardo Castilleja Chávez*
New Delhi: *Ramtanu Maitra*
Paris: *Christine Bierre*
Stockholm: *Ulf Sandmark*
United Nations, N.Y.C.: *Leni Rubinstein*
Washington, D.C.: *William Jones*
Wiesbaden: *Göran Haglund*

ON THE WEB
e-mail: eirns@larouchepub.com
www.larouchepub.com
www.executiveintelligencereview.com
www.larouchepub.com/eiw
Webmaster: *John Sigerson*
Assistant Webmaster: *George Hollis*
Editor, Arabic-language edition: *Hussein Askary*

EIR (ISSN 0273-6314) *is published weekly (50 issues), by EIR News Service, Inc., P.O. Box 17390, Washington, D.C. 20041-0390. (703) 777-9451*

European Headquarters: E.I.R. GmbH, Postfach Bahnstrasse 9a, D-65205, Wiesbaden, Germany Tel: 49-611-73650
Homepage: http://www.eirna.com
e-mail: eirna@eirna.com
Director: Georg Neudecker

Montreal, Canada: 514-461-1557

Denmark: EIR - Danmark, Sankt Knuds Vej 11, basement left, DK-1903 Frederiksberg, Denmark. Tel.: +45 35 43 60 40, Fax: +45 35 43 87 57. e-mail: eirdk@hotmail.com.

Mexico City: EIR, Sor Juana Inés de la Cruz 242-2 Col. Agricultura C.P. 11360
Delegación M. Hidalgo, México D.F.
Tel. (5525) 5318-2301
eirmexico@gmail.com

Now the Hard Road Is the Only Road

Now the Hard Road Is the Only Road

Oct 14—Now, at last, force yourself to face the facts. This bad joke of a nominating process can never produce a Democratic candidate who could be honestly elected by the American people. Hillary Clinton has decided to be,—or has been decided to be,—the candidate of Wall Street. She was already the cheerleader for the Bush-Cheney-Obama wars and murders in Iraq, Libya, and Syria. And Bernie Sanders is now the candidate of the hated Barack Obama, whom he used to attack, but now praises and supports. The corrupt fundraisers for Obama's campaigns, who smuggled in drug-money under cover of anonymous internet contributions in 2008 for Obama's fraudulent victory over a better Hillary Clinton,—have now moved over to perform the same service for Bernie Sanders. (Nothing need be said of the Republican so-called nominating process.)

Such morally-failed candidates, Wall Street and Obama candidates, can do nothing to begin to reverse the destruction the United States has suffered under almost 16 years of murderous Bush-Cheney-Obama tyranny. Rather, they will blast the country to oblivion well before January 2017.

A different nominating process must be begun now, directed not so much to nominating a single individual for President, but much more towards the creation of a Presidential team, like Franklin Roosevelt's or George Washington's team, for example, which unites within itself the qualifications and the knowledge to rescue our country while there is still time. And like Roosevelt's and Washington's teams in their time, that team must be assembled now, in and around Manhattan.

First, to deal with the obvious objection. If you say that that is "impractical," then there is something very important which you yourself must learn right now. Practical people are dead people. The deadness which is already within them, will manifest itself quickly, now, as biological death, unless they renounce "being practical,"—or else, one may hope, are rescued, although through no merit of their own, by the creative people, who are not practical people.

This is what Edgar Allan Poe tried to teach you in his great stories, "The Pit and the Pendulum," and "A Descent into the Maelström," among so many others. Reread them now. Indeed, he sacrificed everything to teach you this; and now, well over a century later, have you learned nothing at all?

This country can only be saved when the great mass of the people take their cue from the few creative people. Only a new Renaissance can save this country now.

A Manhattan Party

Lyndon LaRouche addressed this in a discussion last night.

"It's the Universe that's the issue, at least the human part of the Universe as we know it. And therefore, we're going to have to have a composition pulled together which meets that requirement. And we can do that. If we get our ass off the shelf, shall we say, or something like that, we can do it! And we can do it on the basis of a central reference to Manhattan.

"So what we're going to do is have a Manhattan party. It's called a national re-election party: We're going to center everything around the parts of the nation, on the basis of a single campaign for a new Presidential system. And we're going to get a team to get in there, with no more bullshit. No mere facts, no party lines, no meaningful suggestions, which are sometimes the most rotten ones you can possibly get, in my experience.

"So it has to be a Manhattan-centered orientation, because the key is, as I pointed out earlier: Dump Wall Street! If we don't have a dump Wall Street campaign as the leading course of action, you don't win anything. So we have to say, 'Shut down Wall Street, now, while we can, with Glass-Steagall, we can change the situation with Glass-Steagall.' We can do it. So we have to do it.

"And we get ourselves marching with some real ammunition which we have to pull together, and we're going to turn this thing upside down. It's vulnerable enough that it can be done. The fact is that the two campaigns, as such, the so-called leading campaigns for the Democratic Party have flopped. They're flopped, they're dead, they're finished! So what kind of a Democratic campaign do you have? You don't have a Democratic Party campaign! You have a bastard Republican Party campaign. That's the way you campaign, people like Trump. That's the kind of thing that's being pushed.

"So we have to blow it. And we can blow it on an international basis, although you don't like to usually do that on an international basis in terms of U.S. politics. But this time it's come: What Putin is doing, together with China and India, and about three other nations which are smaller, tied to Putin now, that's a pretty good constituent.

"And the enemy is the British Empire! The competition is with the British Empire! It's in sorry conditions; it's on the edge itself, like Wall Street. Wall Street is hopelessly dead. If you want to be a Wall Streeter, you're a dead person; there's no way that mankind can live under Wall Street, or any form of Wall Street. The very existence of Wall Street will mean its death in panic. And you will get an extinction of most of the human population, as a result of such a panic.

"So the bullshit is *over*.

A Global Perspective

"And that's where we are. We're at a point where as of this moment now, with the package we have as of now, the recent developments which match that right now, we, our campaign policy, is *dead*! Because it is not a campaign policy; it's a wishful thinking policy. And therefore, we have to think about how we are going to assemble something which has got the energy to do something about this. And the way we can do it,—we can do it on the basis of what Putin has done, and what Putin has done is not just Putin; it's China; it's India; it's a whole group of smaller nations, that is, less-weight nations, working together with Putin, and it's there!

"So what you have to do, is you have to operate on the basis of a vision, not of local complexions, not of regional sections, but you've got to think of a global perspective. The old idea of the principle of party is *crap*, and we've just got to get rid of that crappy habit. And we're going to have to start right now on what basis, with the fact that we know something and these guys *don't*. That's the issue. The people who want to be practical are the people who don't know how to think.

"We are now in a question of a planetary crisis. Can the planet as a planet, in and of itself, now sustain an actual institution on planet Earth? And I would say now, 'No.' People pretend it exists, but it actually doesn't. And everything now is on this new kind of process, where you have nations which are defined as nations with sovereignty. But the sovereignty is conditioned, because there are overreaching moral questions which have to be superior to any so-called Constitution....

Take 9/11

"What happened when Manhattan was attacked by the Saudis, when mass murder was occurring in Manhattan, and what has been done by the United States on that issue since that time? I would say that how we deal with this thing should be a leading factor. Because this thing is so raw, right now. The situation is so raw, so degenerated, that opinion itself has become degenerated. Because if you take any part of the community within our nation, you feel like you're dealing with a degenerate; different flavors of degeneracy.

"And therefore, you have to take the right kind of themes; don't think about the political forms *per se*. Think about what happened to the people who got killed by the Saudis and the British: Isn't that a good issue? Isn't that a live issue?

"Jeff [Steinberg] and I had some fun with that issue, in the sense of—you know, knowing the facts, and being guided into an experience together with some British forces who are loyal to people, as opposed to the other variety. We knew this was coming: We knew that the British monarchy did it! And used the Saudis as the instrument. That's what 9/11 was! And I knew it before it happened, and Jeff knew it before it happened! And that should be a little test of,—do you know what the truth of history is?

"And so we take those kinds of issues, not the so-called practical issues, but those kind of issues; and you organize around Classical music, according to the proper principle, which we have an organization for, essentially in Manhattan and around it now. Change the alternative! Change the orientation! Putin I'm sure will join; China I'm sure will join, others. Let's do something about it.

"Now, we've got a breakdown, a total breakdown of the Democratic Party,—totally shattered right now, as of now. And it was obvious to me at midday on Friday, that this thing is dead; the Democratic Party teams were dead."

EIR Contents

www.larouchepub.com Volume 42, Number 41, October 16, 2015

The Twentieth Century Was a Failure Because It Substituted Mathematics for Morality

This exchange between long-time Lyndon LaRouche associates Gerald Rose and Philip Rubinstein was recorded on Oct. 11.

Rose: So, Phil, the question comes up in the most dramatic way possible, with the fact that you now have within the trans-Atlantic system, the combination of what Putin has done, in terms of an actual fight against terrorism in Syria,—a serious fight on the basis of the reality of terrorism,—and his own moral commitments to Russia and the defense of the whole of humanity, which he himself learned personally through his family commitments, during the Nazi siege of Leningrad [now St Petersburg]. And he will not be deterred. And the Obama reaction, as we know, has been completely insane, in terms of a spiralling out-of-control of the kinds of provocations that he's capable of and committed to.

But on the whole, as LaRouche identified, you compare the U.S. leadership, which is disgusting, even to the morality which has come forth in Germany in response to the refugee crisis. You have a certain reaction by Merkel to just a fundamental moral question of whether you're just going to murder people, and throw them onto the scrapheap; and her response, and the German people's response, is: We're not going to do that. But you could not get such a response within the United States as it is now currently existing.

And what LaRouche put on the table is the problem is that the ideology of the Twentieth Century doesn't function. The Twentieth Century has replaced morality by mathematics, and what we want to discuss, and what I want you to elaborate, is: what do you think that means? How do we go at such a question?

Rubinstein: Well, I think we have to get to a fairly

Theoretical option price $= pN(d_1) - se^{-rt}N(d_2)$

where $d_1 = \dfrac{\ln\left(\frac{p}{s}\right) + \left(r + \frac{v^2}{2}\right)t}{v\sqrt{t}}$

$d_2 = d_1 - v\sqrt{t}$

The variables are:

p = stock price

s = striking price

t = time remaining until expiration, expressed as a percent of a year

r = current risk-free interest rate

v = volatility measured by annual standard deviation

$\ln$ = natural logarithm

$N(x)$ = cumulative normal density function

creative commons/ Richard Drew

The frenzy of the New York Stock Exchange, and the sophisticated mathematical models of competitive advantage go together more intimately than you know. The market scene is from Sept. 17, 2008.

deep level. First of all, I think most people will immediately respond, why mathematics? Because to a large extent people don't understand what runs their lives, and they have been dumbed down to the point that they don't even ask the question any more.

Indeed, look at Wall Street! Wall Street is essentially based—and we may come back to this—they talk about free market theory, but it's basically a mathematical game. Game theory. A zero sum game, and the idea is to come up with some advantage out of it, and that's what most of the investments, and the investment strategies and the direction that people get, is based on.

Mathematical game theory: what moves gain you a little bit versus what somebody else loses: what raises the prices; what do people like; how do they feel about things. It has nothing to do with economics. It's a mathematical construct really of the Twentieth Century.

Hilbert's 1900 Project

You had free market theory with Adam Smith before, but the idea that you could mathematically express the value, the monetary value, the paper value, because of what people's likes and dislikes are, is largely a Twentieth Century addition. And that's what the whole derivatives flow out of Wall Street is based on. You know: Can I get somebody to place a bet on the value of a financial instrument, and how can I rig the game so that I make something off of the bet? And how can I then bet upon the bet? You say that and people get all freaked out, but that's what's going on.

This is the nature of—Take health care: You notice now that most of these doctors, or paramedics, walk around with little tablets or versions of computers, and you tell them you've got a pain on your left side, and they punch in some things on the computer with your medical record, and they come up with some kind of evaluation of whether or not you should be treated, or how much you should be treated. And this is all based on actuarial charts that the insurance companies utilize.

So, this whole idea that you could numerically evaluate and express scientific knowledge, reached an apex in the Twentieth Century, and this was done quite consciously at the end of the Nineteenth Century, as has been identified, by David Hilbert and Bertrand Russell. And in some ways—the background of these men to

start with: for the purposes of this, I want to emphasize Hilbert's role. Russell is an evil character; he hates human beings, and so on.

But Hilbert put forward the project that you could axiomatize science—physics, chemistry. But I'll tell you the axiomatization project—you know, he had 23 propositions to be solved, some of them technical, mathematical, that in and of themselves would not make that much of an impact, but the idea was that the *truth*, science, was to be achieved through simply mathematics.

And then Hilbert's own version of this—whether he was the kind of character Russell was, I don't know, but he was the spokesman for this—even his idea of mathematics was a degraded version. It was pure formalism: it was the idea that really the content of events,—the content of the real Universe,—doesn't matter, because the only way you can reach certain truth is by the formal relations, the logical relations, within whatever idea you have.

So, he says, for example, that he could take Euclidean geometry, which is problematic anyway, and in effect, he wanted to do with geometry at that point what Euclid did to ancient geometry, which was constructive, which was a kind of truthful practice—Euclid turned it into an axiomatic system. At the end of the Nineteenth Century, it was known that Euclidean geometry was *not* the geometry of the Universe—and we can come back to that a little bit later.

But what does Hilbert attempt to do? He says, we can axiomatize in a purely formal sense any version of geometry. And he says, for example: I can replace point, line, and plane with coffee, cup, and sugar, and I could replace them for point, line, and plane, and give you a completely consistent formal system. And that's the way we ought to effectively do everything.

From that standpoint, he laid out the project later on of proving that mathematics—arithmetic as a basis of all mathematics—could be axiomatized, and then proven to be perfectly consistent in the sense of never proving a contradiction, and complete. And so the foundations of our knowledge would be secure.

Now, this completely leaves out any fundamental new ideas. It rules out human creativity. It rules out the human mind. And that's what really plays itself out in physics: not so much with simply some of the perplexing features of physics, but the idea that once you have the math, you don't need to get reality. You don't need to get what's really out there. This is what Einstein opposed, contrary to the way he's often described. It wasn't determinism; it was the idea that you couldn't discover reality, and then act on it for the betterment of the human species.

When you take creativity out, in a very precise way—not just any arbitrary innovation—because what LaRouche did in his physical economics, and that's what I think we mean by reality here, what LaRouche demonstrated is that the human species depends on creativity—that is, progress in our knowledge of the Universe. That's what makes us unique as a species. We evolve ourselves through the creative development of our relationship to the Universe in the form of knowledge that gets us deeper into the Universe. But that's necessary to human existence. It gives meaning to human life.

Philosopher in Meditation, painted by Rembrandt in 1632. Just where does the hypothesis come from?

Creativity is Knowable

Because human beings live with the reality that they're going to die, which can be a bit of an unsettling sense. But we also live with the knowledge, or should, that we can contribute to what is an eternal, effectively, future for the human species, because we are creators, as the Creator of the Universe, the Composer, if you want to express it that way. But I really want to leave it, that we know how to create within this Universe, relations to the Universe that expand our ability as a species.

If you rule real science out, that kind of development, you have no morality. You have no ability to organize the human species to a common purpose that's going to improve future species, in which each generation of youth can look forward to a deeper and more profound future for the generations that follow them, and to improve upon and develop those that preceded them.

So the human species has the capability of being what Schiller called sublime: facing the mortality of every creature—human beings being conscious of that reality, but we can overcome it.

Hilbert's program,—of course, Russell picked it up—basically made the effort to axiomatize arithmetic as the basis for all science, because of the idea that science bases its truth on its mathematical precision. One of the things that you'll get is that: what is science? It's induction, experience, then you run into problems; you do more, and you come up with a hypothesis, and then you test the hypothesis.

Well, one of the real problems in this is, where does the hypothesis come from? Most of these guys just skip over it. In fact, it's a mystery. Some of them are actually quite mystical, despite being positivists, as Russell was. They say, well, that's just completely unknown; it just happens. It's just arbitrary. Whereas the others, including people like Einstein and Planck, and others before them—Leibniz and Lyn [Lyndon LaRouche] and people today, if they're very advanced, will say, "No. Creativity is something that is intelligible, even if it's not easily expressed. It can't be expressed in any formal way, but it is something that is knowable, and can be done with a certain sense of intention, at least from a social standpoint."

So, what happened at the end of the Nineteenth Century then played itself out in the destruction of the breakthroughs that were made. We had the development of nuclear physics at the end of the Nineteenth Century. We had the expansion of our knowledge of the Universe through Einstein's development of special and general relativity, and the beginning of knowledge about galactic relationships. Greater universal developments. All of this in front of us approximately in 1900.

By the 1920s and '30s, this was not only under attack, but had been largely undermined with the idea—and these were followers of Russell. People like Max Born, and Heisenberg. Heisenberg, for example, says that there's only the observations, when indeed Planck and Einstein had demonstrated that the observations were completely inadequate. This is what Born says. And these were followers of Russell. Neils Bohr was one.

Then you had the development of computers, artificial intelligence, which I think is a whole other story. A lot of what we see today as the collapse of morality, is the fact that we educate people on computers; we babysit them with computers; we consider computers to be intelligent, when they represent nothing but a formalism that can be put to good use, and is capable of doing rather remarkable things in aid of human knowledge, but it is *not* intelligence; it's not human; it's not creativity, and we've dumbed down the population by effectively giving them the idea that they are inferior, except perhaps in some expressions of emotion, to computers.

What LaRouche has fought since the end of World War II is this idea of artificial intelligence, information theory, game theory, and presented an entirely different morality, which can be in some way expressed in what he calls increased energy flux density, which itself depends on discovery of new universal principles, and expressed in relative potential population density. So you have a certain forecast, but it's expressed in a qualitative development of the human species.

Russell as a Young Beast-Man

Rose: Well, Phil, you know, the question is how much was this Russell-Hilbert program a reaction in fact to the breakout of science in terms of Riemann,

One of Bertrand Russell's arch-enemies, German scientist and philosopher Gottfried Leibniz, shown in his statue on the exterior of the Royal Academy of Arts in London.

Pasteur, the whole ferment at the end of the Nineteenth Century?

Rubinstein: Certainly in Russell's case, he absolutely—and in fact, there's a simple proof of it—picking up your point. Because really, you had Gauss and Riemann—let's just take those two in the early and mid-Nineteenth Century. And they made enormous breakthroughs. And in fact, I'll say ironically, breakthroughs that expressed themselves in an entirely expanded new capability to express a mathematical language that's far superior to what existed before.

They developed the complex domain. They developed Riemann's conception of Riemann surfaces, and anti-Euclidean geometry, as he expresses in his famous Habilitation paper, where he ended by saying, I think, for 1700 years we haven't understood the basis of our geometry. Now we're going to express that, and he concludes by saying, ultimately you have to go to the realm of real physical science to answer what is the geometry of the physical Universe.

And he developed the conception of Riemann surfaces, which is a conception of ongoing, in a way, ongoing development. It has a certain technical mathematical side, but it's a way of expressing ideas that could never before be expressed in mathematics. And in fact, Riemann is often accused of not being rigorous enough, but he proves, by being a scientist, everything that he says. In many ways, the same goes for Gauss, who was a little bit less open about what he was doing.

Now these breakthroughs allowed us to expand the development of electro-magnetism, the development of nuclear physics, and so on and so forth. People like Planck and Einstein depended—Planck in his own way; Einstein had to sort of go to Riemann to find a mathematics strong enough to express his ideas. And of course, this brought us—as you say, at the end of the

Nineteenth Century, here there was an entirely new Universe, a new Universe of quantum physics, of nuclear physics, understanding the continuum and the discreteness was open to us. We had breakthroughs in health, as you pointed out, by Pasteur, but also the beginnings of knowledge about biology. People like Vernadsky are working in Russia, later the Soviet Union, on these same areas.

This is what LaRouche built his whole conception of economics off of. It goes back further, but we don't have time to go into everything: Leibniz, and so on, and Kepler, and so forth. But let's just focus on this. So, what happens is Russell, as a relatively young guy, but a member of the aristocracy, and a person who hated human beings—his whole life was dedicated to hating. He hated scientific development. He hated industry. He hated the United States. He hated the industrial development of the Soviet Union; he promoted the backwardness that he saw in China.

But as a young man in the 1890s, two of the things that he does before the infamous *Principia Mathematica*, is he wrote *A History of Western Philosophy*, and he basically attacks Leibniz. He says that Leibniz was really a logician. Don't take seriously his metaphysical side, his idea of the best of all possible worlds, his idea of the monad—this is all B.S. to get him in good with oligarchy, and he's basically a logician.

And of course, in his *Foundation for Geometry*, Russell also mocks Riemannian geometry. He says you can't really have anything but Euclidean geometry in the actual physical Universe. So, he's deployed against human progress. His whole idea in the *Principia* is to prove that there is no real purpose in the human mind. It can all be axiomatized, and everything else is pure feelings, pure sensory experience.

Now, Hilbert—I'm less clear on Hilbert as a personality—he's clearly weak on a lot of things. Actually I think what you have is, in Göttingen, you have this whole mathematizing school: Felix Klein. Related to it, Minkowsky, who does some perhaps useful things, but is not a valid expression of special relativity. Weierstrass, who's not a good one, but they all attack Riemann for not being formal enough.

For example, his whole idea of Riemann surfaces is rejected. The Dirichlet principle is rejected. They insist on various forms of algebraic formulations that Riemann had superseded. So you have a clear attack on these potential breakthroughs. And in fact, Göttingen

and other people related to Göttingen play a very big role in the mathematizing of quantum theory. Born, in particular; Sommerfeld wasn't there, but he's working with these guys. And by the late 1920s, they're basically arguing that we have no way of expressing reality. We have the mathematical formulas. And really, a lot of physics since then has been not unlike the Ptolemaic or Copernican theory, where you can add an epicycle to make the mathematics work, and cover the data, but you can never know what's real. It's only the mathematics.

This is what came out of the 1927 and 1930 Solvay conferences that Einstein fought so valiantly against, and maybe I can come back to that.

Riemann

So, I think that Lyn's point, that Russell was evil, the most evil man of the Twentieth Century—this is a guy who on at least a dozen different occasions after World War II, raised the issue of pre-emptive nuclear bombing of the Soviet Union. Later on he tried to claim that he hadn't said that, but in 1953, a letter was produced in which he says, we want to h-bomb the Soviet Union. And his own biographer said, look, there were at least a dozen times—in various interviews, letters—where Russell expressed this. He only became anti-nuclear, a peacenik again, after the Soviet Union got the hydrogen bomb. He'd been a pacifist for World War I, but that was really part of a whole orientation of the British oligarchy to reorganize the Empire.

So, he was a creature of the British Empire to the marrow of his bones, and to the inside of every cell of his being.

Rose: Let me ask you, Phil. The reason I asked the Riemann question is because when Lyn describes his own breakthrough, this fundamental scientific discovery,—which is really one of the dominant revolutions going on in the BRICS, expressed in many different ways,—he describes it as "LaRouche-Riemann," really going back to before the whole mathematical formalism which dominated the Twentieth Century.

Why did Lyn say "LaRouche-Riemann?"

Rubinstein: I think Riemann really makes the breakthrough that takes geometry, mathematics, outside of this formal realm. Because what does he say in his *Habilitation* paper? And you see it in some of what Riemann discovered: his work on tensor analysis, which is basically, to put it in—I don't know every technical detail, but the idea is that you're dealing with a multiple changing set of dimensions, or principles, really. A multiple set of interacting principles. Not a three-dimensional Pythagorean system. You're dealing with all kinds of potential universal principles—gravity, electromagnetism, stresses, shearing factors, electrical circuits, and so forth and so on, and you can develop an idea of how to, in effect, act on things that have multiple dimensions. Not dimensions really, but multiple principles acting.

So, this is a totally different language. It's probably the closest thing to poetry that—this is why you need poetry to supercede mathematics. Because you have to think poetically to have this kind of an idea.

Now Riemann surfaces have the same character. But the way he expresses this is by saying, we don't know the geometry that we think we know, because Euclidean axioms have never been demonstrated. They're just accepted.

What's the real science, what's the real Universe that we live in? And it's this kind of constant sense of development that Lyn sees—as I said, this is the morality of the human species when it's being truly human. Science and morality are intimately bound together, contrary to what people believe now. What do they believe today? There's reality, which we have no real way of knowing, and then we have these mathematical expressions that allow us to utilize things we otherwise don't understand.

And morality is not expressed in mathematics. Morality is not expressed in a formal system. Truth there, is merely the ability to manipulate symbols.

So you have a dichotomy in the Universe. You have a human being and his feelings, which are effectively outside the Universe. Lyn says the human species is part of what the Universe has created. The Universe has created a creative species, and our existence depends on

EIRNS/Stuart Lewis

Lyndon LaRouche's seminal economic textbook, published in 1984.

that creativity. That's the morality that we express to other members of the human species, and in our relationship to the Universe.

So I think that Riemann is the culmination of the work of people like Gauss, Leibniz, and Kepler, and so in part, we point to him as in many ways the last full representative of that. And Lyn himself is using that to go beyond it. You had some developments by Planck and Einstein and Vernadsky, but ultimately in the Twentieth Century, Einstein stands alone as the one figure who says, "I don't accept this reign of mathematics, formalism, positivism. We as human beings, need to know that we can know the Universe."

So-Called Artificial Intelligence

As I said, Einstein's often accused of wanting to be a Classical scientist, in promoting determinism—that we have no freedom, no creativity. That's not true. He says over and over again that science is based on creativity. What he's saying, is what's Classical is that the human species can know the Universe. And what we have so far, as an interpretation of quantum theory and certain other problems, is not a knowledge of reality. It's the use of a mathematical formalism and substituting that for reality.

That's why science has stopped. No one is creating a real new science, new breakthroughs based on what we've done through the Nineteenth Century. They'll talk about a new physics, but all they mean is adding an epicycle to what's going on now.

However, I do think these concerns to create even that, reflect the problems in the science—the stagnation of it.

Rose: This comes up very dramatically on this question of "can computers think." Anyone who says that, or who thinks that, is falling into the horror of the Twentieth Century. Because the question—and I'd like you to elaborate a little more—this question of the super-Turing machine, this idea that von Neumann and others have come up with, is this question of game theory. And the idea that the future is somehow projectable from the present—it seems to me that that's the horror and the absolute entropy and destruction that they impose upon the human species. Can you comment on that?

Rubinstein: Well, I think it's an interesting case. I mean, human beings are not like any animal, and they're not like any machine. And Lyn has discussed this extensively. What animal even knows that it's going to die? You get a lot of this approximation. You know, they do this, they do that. They don't come close! You look at what the human species has developed,—even with all its problems,—the genuine progress of the human species, and there's nothing in the animal world that touches it, even an infinite approximation.

Now, you had this phenomenon in the Twentieth Century of machines, artificial intelligence, computers. Now people have sometimes tried to run calculator machines in the past—fine. Actually, one of the things that generated this fascination with computers is a lot of technology developed off the scientific breakthroughs of over 100 years ago. Nuclear physics, atomic physics, electro-magnetism, and so on and so forth. So we're able to do things at a very high speed with new materials and so forth.

But what really, what the core of this is—there's an interesting case, and they made a movie about this guy Alan Turing, "The Imitation Game." And partly he helped to break the German codes in World War II, and then he had this thing called the Turing test: Could you distinguish between the machine and a human being—could you create a machine that imitated a human being sufficiently so that you couldn't tell the difference?

Now, I won't go into the craziness of that, but I will say one thing. First of all, the idea that they make him into some kind of a hero who saved—this is how the British saved the world, basically. He comes from a

British computer scientist and mathematician Alan Turing (1912-1954).

family of British civil servants, who served mainly in India; he didn't, but that is somewhat his education and his background. So the idea that he saved everybody from World War II is an absurdity, but it's the kind of thing that people get fascinated by,—he broke the code.

Now, the second thing about him, which made him somewhat of a hero, because he was a homosexual who was certainly undoubtedly persecuted at the end of his life, and it may have been partly because he was the bearer of certain secrets. But anyway, he basically took upon himself part of the project that Hilbert had put forward; that is, he wanted to answer some of these questions about the foundations of mathematics after Gödel.

Gödel had proven that Russell's system was neither consistent, nor complete—or, if you tried to make it consistent, there would be truths that you couldn't prove. And if you tried to make complete, it would be inconsistent. But there was another question that Hilbert raised, which was: Can you tell, given a given formula, can you decide by some mechanical finite means, some mechanism, something mechanical step-by-step, approaching what they call a recursive function of some kind,—can you decide with a finite number of steps whether it's true or not?

Now, ironically enough, Turing proved that,—just like the Gödel's proof,—no! In other words, the machine might go on forever. If you gave it a certain problem, and it just kept going, you couldn't tell whether it would solve it or not. So you could run into that kind of serious problem, a limitation on any mechanical system.

Computer Religion

But in the course of doing that, he came up with an idea called the "universal Turing machine." Now what's the principle that he uses in this?

His principle is: it's not in the content. In other words, you can run a problem through the machine, and the machine has instructions on how to deal with the problem, how to deal with the calculation. And be-

cc/Tom Yates

A complete and working replica of the Turing machine at the National Codes Centre at Bletchley Park, site of the UK's Government Code and Cypher School during World War II.

cause you can vary the instructions, you can put anything through the machine. And if it's calculable by mechanical means, the machine can do it. Therefore, it's a universal Turing machine. It's an idea. Nobody would ever build such a thing, because it would be massively cumbersome—it only has a huge number of steps—but every computer can be reduced, so to speak, to a Turing machine. It can be broken down into a Turing machine.

Now, Turing was also certainly a very funny guy. Now they say he might have been autistic. I think he just had certain social limitations. And his view was, he would refer to the machine, looking at the tape going through it, he would refer to that as a state of mind. From his standpoint, the machine was equivalent to human intelligence, or even a mind. He was particularly far gone on some of this. But this is the basic outlook.

John von Neumann. A very strange personality, but the same point. They were both sort of these kinds of *idiots savant*—in certain areas they could solve problems very easily, but they were socially limited. But anyway, I think even if they weren't socially limited, Turing's whole view was everything was in the instructions. Everything was in the operating system, and you could change the instructions, and he even had some idea that the machine could learn, because you could have some algorithm that told you when to change the instructions.

Basically, it's the software. So for Turing, and all these people, what's the software? It's formal logical systems. It's a simple binary code with a kind of "if-then" system of logic built into it. The reason it's binary is that you can make it "yes" or "no." It's basically truth tables, or truth trees. And the idea he had,—he didn't argue that that was the human brain, but he said that it could do everything that human intelligence could do.

Now with the added velocities of these machines in the ensuing 70 years… And these guys talk about this—Claude Shannon at Bell Labs with his information theory,—somebody that LaRouche polemicized against,—John von Neumann, Norbert Wiener—in various ways they all believed that this logical system was a system that could carry out all mathematical functions,—that this was human intelligence, which is the measure of truth.

And that's really where it comes in. Yes, human beings can have feelings. They can be conscious. But where is truth? Truth is in this kind of mechanical system.

I'll give you one funny story. When Turing met Shannon, one of the things that they discussed was what they could do with their machinery. Turing went on to point out that he imagined feeding in facts on prices of commodities and stock, while asking the machine the question, should I buy or sell? This is in 1940 or so when Turing is in the United States. So, you get an idea of the way these guys think. And this is exactly what has demoralized and degraded the population.

And I personally think that it's not just that it's the stock market, but that it's the way science is treated—most science students today, they don't do science. They do computer modeling. But beyond that, if you

A young child glued to the internet.

take 15, 14 year olds, 16 year olds, and they're glued to a digital system, and they're communicating through digital systems, with all the limitations and the restrictions and the way you have to go through the loops, you're destroying their mind. You're destroying their emotions; you're destroying their personality; you're destroying their minds.

And it's very interesting. The UN had a report which referred to some work that Helga and others have done on the fact that many of these shooters, so-called—I think almost all of them (I haven't seen the report)—are video game players, or computer game players. Now, the argument is,—not everybody on a computer becomes a killer. Fine, that may be true, but it may also up the likelihood. But I think it's a good insight into what computers do to the human minds of children going through the process of development of their creative capabilities.

Math vs. Morality

Rose: Just finally, because I think what you've painted is a devastating picture of what's happened in the Twentieth Century—even more fleshed out as a result of Hilbert and Russell. We've discussed this often with Lyn on the question of what is morality. The question of morality is the commitment to the future. Now most people think of the future in absolute space-time, right? As a projection of the present, and making it a little better, or something.

The real breakthrough of Lyn, but also very dramatically Einstein, is that—and I want your comment on this—is this question of, where exactly is the future? It is the basis for morality. Everything else is somewhat romantic.

Rubinstein: I would say, to utilize somewhat what LaRouche has put forward—it might not be up to the standard but—let's put it this way. Morality, creativity, and the future are really equivalent. Once you take the future out, from a mathematical standpoint, everything is a tautology. Then what you get in the Twentieth Century also, some other things like this guy Wittgenstein, who ultimately says, well, everything is a tautology. There's no content in the formalisms, and then he says, everything is a game, a language. In fact, there are other forms of this.

But morality, real creativity, is the creation of the future. You're creating something that doesn't exist today. The human species does things that never happened in the Universe before, at least in any part of the Universe that we've had contact with.

So we develop nuclear physics. We're doing things at the nuclear level that don't happen in nature by itself; we do it in densities, or we do it in transformations. There are the ultra-uranic elements of the periodic table. We've done with electricity and electromagnetism things that open up the Universe, leading us to discover more of it. And we find out that there's ever more, and ever more to discover.

Because we're changing our relationship to the Universe, we're changing our experiences, we're changing what happens in the Universe. So, we're minimally changing the future, in a sense, as an addition to the creation that the Universe has produced thus far. And that's the basis upon which the human species distinguishes itself; the way in which—we don't survive by doing the same thing over and over again. We survive by reproducing a higher level of knowledge that gives us greater power in the Universe, and makes each individual more valuable.

We reject monetarism. That's Lyn's morality. That's the morality of the American System at its best, of Hamilton, that we've pointed to. So, creativity, morality, science—and what you also see, is something else.

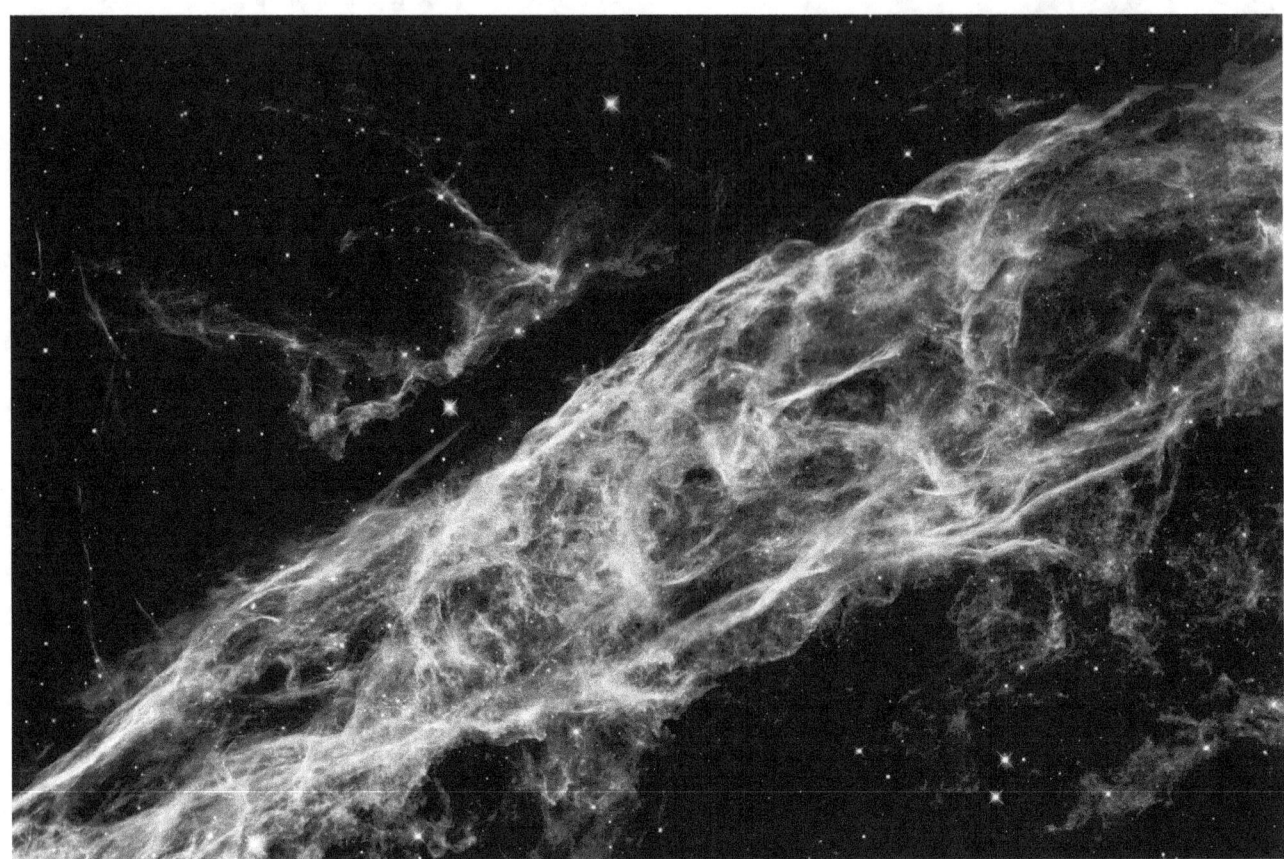

A Hubble telescope image of the Veil Nebula, released on Sept. 24, 2015.

The place where we can express creativity in a more direct way, is in the so-called Classical arts. Classical composition that bases itself on expressing creativity—and that's the morality of art.

You also saw the change at the end of the Nineteenth Century in music. Brahms died in 1897. And what do you have in the Twentieth Century? A mathematization of what's supposed to be the new Classical music. Serial music, atonal music. What is this? It's a mathematical formula for composing music. And then you get, of course, in the wildness—I'm not talking about popular music *per se*, but that gets worse and worse. And then, of course, you get wild stuff like John Cage—4 minutes and 33 seconds of noise, which is of the trash man playing in the background.

But this is the same thing. It's all one piece.

So, creativity is not arbitrary. In other words, we face certain problems; we know certain things that we have to improve our knowledge of and expand; we know things that we have to do, like go out into the Solar System; we know that we have to know more about the Galaxy, because that's where we're situated. And indeed it's the processes of development of the Universe as a whole that are even reflected in the small.

So, we know we have sorts of tests for the imagination. We develop our skills at looking at the way in which ideas evolve and develop, the ways in which paradoxes occurred that have to be subsumed. This idea of the *coincidentia oppositorum*. This isn't just bridging contradictions; it's demonstrating that there are two apparently anomalous and contradictory things in the existing Universe, which are in one Universe. They have to be resolved, and there's a higher level resolution.

Where do all our ideas about the infinite come from?

So, one of the things that Lyn is saying, when he says morality has been replaced by mathematics,—because if you destroy science, and you destroy the future, you've destroyed morality. You're immoral.

Book Review

Discoveries of a Non-Reductionist

by Liona Fan Chiang

Cosmophysical Factors in Stochastic Processes
by Simon E. Shnoll
Rehoboth, New Mexico: American Research
Press, 2012
Translated by Alexey V. Agafonov and Olga
Seraya from the original Russian edition of 2009,
433 pages, available online at: http://shnoll.
ptep-online.com/publications/shnoll2012.pdf

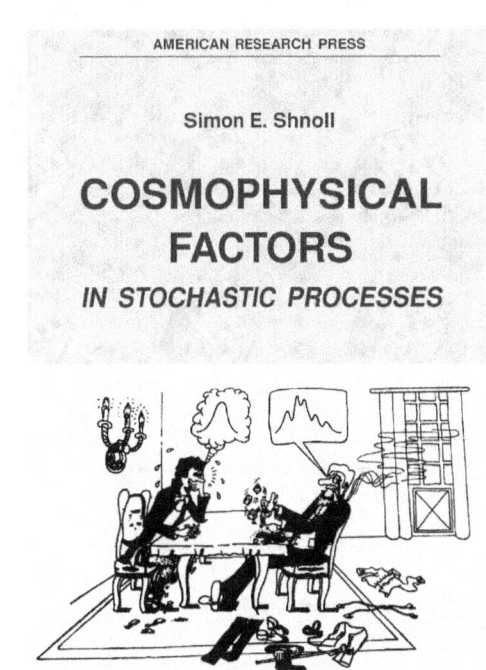

AMERICAN RESEARCH PRESS

Simon E. Shnoll

COSMOPHYSICAL
FACTORS
IN STOCHASTIC PROCESSES

Oct. 11—The journey of Simon El'evich Shnoll—today a professor of physics at Moscow State University—started at the beginning of the atomic age in 1951, when he was employed to prepare radioactive solutions in a "branch of the Atomic Project," the newly reorganized Department of Medical Radiology at the Central Institute for Physician Excellence in Moscow. On the side, at the end of the workday, he performed experiments in his specialty field, biochemistry.

He began with experiments measuring enzymatic (ATPase) activity—the use of ATP by the proteins of the actomyosin complex, a complex that controls muscle contraction—and noticed something strange. The reaction rate seemed to change dramatically over short periods of time. Having taken a measurement of reaction rates every 15 seconds, he found that the rate of reaction did not fluctuate about a particular average rate, but rather varied wildly, sometimes smoothing out and sometimes jumping by a factor of two.

The amount of variation of the reaction rate seemed sporadic, but it was not random. The rates were discrete. When the rates themselves were tracked, it could be seen that there were preferred values. There were also, anomalously, rates which never occurred; they were "forbidden." In an attempt to see if the discreteness would disappear, he eventually increased the number of measurements to hundreds, yet, the discrete-

---

ATP and ATPase:
What Are They?

The adenosine triphosphate molecule (ATP) is widely used in the body to transport energy. ATP is broken down—releasing the energy needed for other specific biochemical reactions locally in parts of the body (such as muscles)—by several enzymes collectively called ATPases.

FIGURE 1

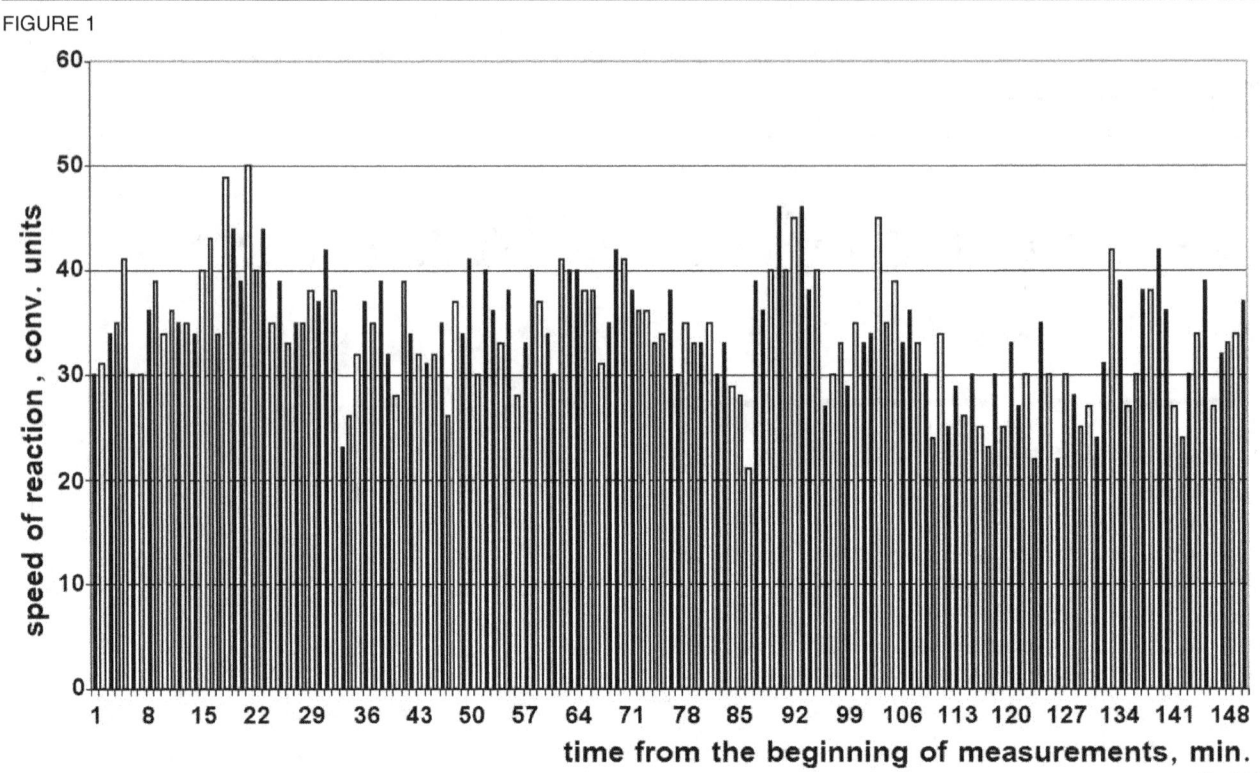

Original Caption: Figure 1-3. Illustration of "macroscopic fluctuations" reaction rates of ATP + creatine → creatine phosphate + ADP catalyzed by the enzyme creatine kinase. Experiment on May 30, 1978. The x-axis displays the time in minutes, and the y-axis the reaction rate in conventional units.

FIGURE 2

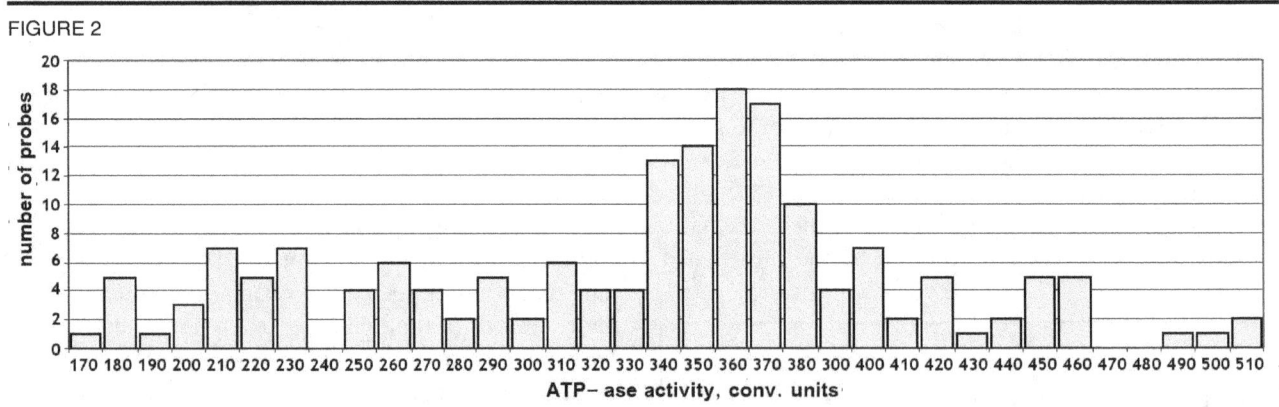

Original Caption: Figure 1-2. The histogram distribution of realized values of the experiment depicted in Fig. 1-1 [omitted], conducted on October 5, 1957.

ness would not disappear; instead it became more distinct. (**Figure 1**)

Figure 2 shows a bar graph (histogram) of these rates. It tabulates the number of times each reaction rate occurred. As can be seen in the graph, the reaction rate of 360 units of ATPase activity per unit of time occurred most frequently, while the rate of 240 units was never registered.

It took several more experiments to prove that the recorded changes in enzyme activity were due to changes in the state, or conformation, of many proteins on a macroscale. In other words, though the proteins are

FIGURE 3

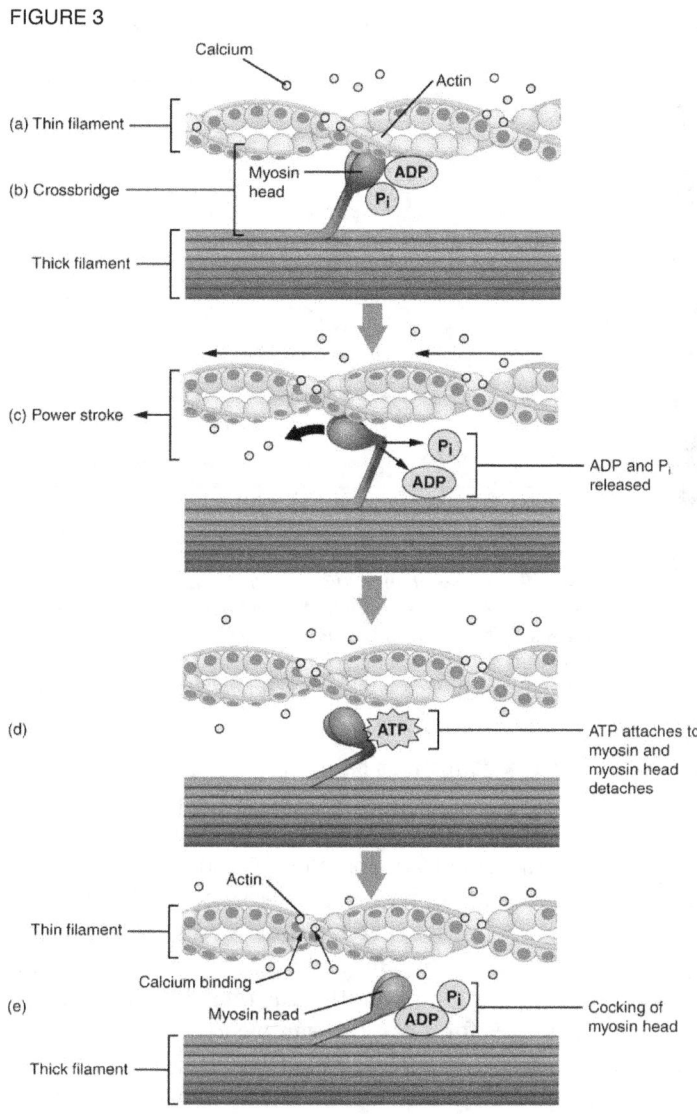

Anatomy & Physiology, an OpenStax College textbook,
http://cnx.org/content/col11496/1.6/, June 19, 2013, unit 2-6-4.

States of conformation in the actin myosin complex in skeletal muscle contraction. ADP is adenosine diphosphate; P_i is inorganic phosphate.

expected to exist in several almost equiprobable states, and individual molecules change conformation rather quickly (10^{-7} seconds), yet somehow a form of synchronization was occurring, manifested as a macroscopic effect (the rate of activity). They were "synchronous in macrovolume," according to Shnoll. (**Figure 3**)

Persistent Synchronicity

In an attempt to narrow down possible causes and factors of influence, Shnoll took measurements from various parts of the volume. He found the same changes in reaction rate. He even took a common solution and poured it into several vials and measured those at the same time. The conformation changes were still synchronized. That is, though the rates continued to fluctuate, seemingly erratically, those fluctuations occurred at the same time for each separate sample.

He tested this repeatedly, spending years trying to detect all possible errors: fluctuations in mechanics, temperature, pressure, and so on. Nothing turned up.

He had a hypothesis: Perhaps it was this synchronization that allows rhythmic patterns in muscle contraction like the wing motion of insects. It was soon disproved, however, when Elizaveta Pavlovna Chetverikova discovered the same fluctuations in an enzyme she was working with, creatine kinase, not a fibril, but a compact globular protein, not related to muscle contraction. Again the reaction rates fluctuated, and they fluctuated synchronously among her samples as well as with his ATPase reactions. Shnoll and Chetverikova then tried every protein they could get their hands on: creatine kinase, pyruvate kinase, alkaline phosphatase, lactic dehydrogenase, acetylcholinesterase, and tripsin. All showed the same synchronicity.

Could it be some fundamental property of biotic processes?

In order to make sure that what he was seeing was indeed an enzymatic reaction, and not due to some merely chemical property during the reaction, he performed what he thought would be a control experiment. He measured the reaction rate of acetic acid with dichrolophenolindophenol (DCPIP, a blue dye), a purely chemical reaction. The reaction turns the solution from blue to clear, making the rate of reaction very easy to track and making detection easy to automate. From these experiments, Shnoll found that although the amplitude of changes in reaction rate was lower, the shape of the histograms could not be distinguished from that of the enzyme reactions.

This meant that either (1) a chemical reaction was influencing the enzyme reactions, but enzymes are just more sensitive to these changes, or (2) the chemical reaction was separately undergoing the same fluctuations of rates; that is, the histograms were the same shape, although the amplitude of variation in rates (Figure 1) is process dependent.

FIGURE 4

Comprehensive Solar Wind Laboratory at Goddard Space Flight Center,
http://lepmfi.gsfc.nasa.gov

Shown here is the heliospheric current sheet which separates positive and negative sides of the the interplanetary magnetic field. Since it is not flat, the Earth crosses from positive to negative sides of the field many times a year.

Finding Exogenous Causes

Shnoll looked for external effects that could impact all reactions. This took many years. He and his collaborators searched for temperature, pressure, pH, mechanical, and several other possible effects. After eliminating these mechanical, thermodynamic, and chemical causes, he found that magnetic and electromagnetic fields influenced the amplitudes of both protein (e.g., enzyme) and chemical reactions.

When 25 years of data were compared to solar activity, the amplitude of scattering (the range of variation of rates) was directly correlated with the rate of change of solar activity, as measured by Wolf number (also known as the international sunspot number).

That is, regardless of the particular level of solar activity at any time, the more quickly the level of solar activity changed, the larger the jumps in enzyme or chemical reaction rate. Amplitude variation was also seen to be influenced by changes in the ionosphere (Layer F2). It was even found to be influenced by the interplanetary magnetic field, increasing two days before the Earth made a sector crossing of the interplanetary magnetic field from positive to negative. (**Figure 4**)

It was clear that changes in amplitude of variation could be influenced by many factors, however the cause of the similarity of histogram shape was still not clear. To investigate the shape of the histograms, Shnoll first tried to find a completely random process

FIGURE 5

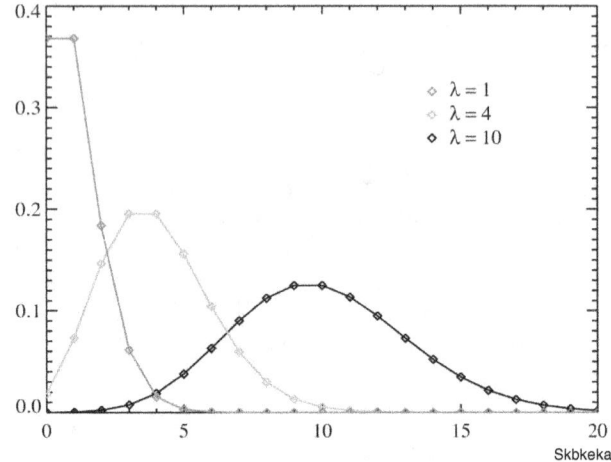

Skbkekas

Poisson distributions for a supposedly ideal stochastic process. Because the process being studied is truly random, the curves become increasingly smooth as the number of measurements increases. The x-axis shows the numbers of occurrences that can happen in the given unit of time; the y-axis shows the probability (frequency) of the different numbers of occurrences happening.

to use as a control, as calibration.

Radioactive decay from one nuclear species to another, which he measured for 10 years as a doctoral student, is accepted as a completely random process in the small. But it has been a puzzle since its discovery in 1896 by Henri Becquerel, for many reasons. One is that it is both very constant and yet very erratic. Each isotope has a distinct, overall decay rate, its half-life, or the time it takes for half of the sample to decay. This rate is immutable. The only way to change it, besides dramatically changing its space-time, is by transforming it into something else, another isotope, which has a different unique half-life.

Yet, despite this predictable characteristic, the exact time at which any particular atom will undergo decay is considered to be completely random and unknowable. Any particular atom may decay right away or years hence.[1] Radioactive decay, therefore, is a process that only has order statistically, macroscopically, and is therefore a truly stochastic process—or so Shnoll had believed—it was "evident a priori."

The histogram of a truly stochastic process is a Poisson distribution. (**Figure 5**) The more measurements in the experiment,. the smoother the curve becomes.

---

1. This randomness was used in the famous Schrödinger's Cat problem, and has even been suggested to be used as a random number generator.

FIGURE 6

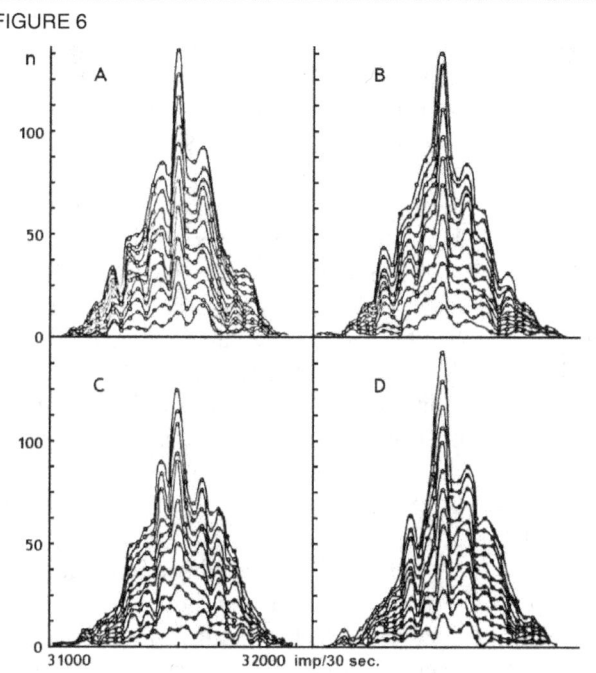

Shnoll 2012

Figure 5-17. The "layered" histograms constructed from the results of measurements of radioactivity of ^{55}Fe on 18-22 February 1982. "Layer lines" are drawn after every set of 100 measurements have been added without any shifting or smoothing. On the x-axis, radioactivity [in imp/30 seconds] is shown and the y-axis shows the number of the measurements of the corresponding value interval of radioactivity.

Radioactivity: A Huge Surprise

Shnoll and his staff ran parallel, simultaneous measurements of carbon-14 radioactive decay in Moscow, and of the creatine kinase (enzyme) reaction in Pushchino, more than 60 miles south of Moscow, and found two astonishing results. First, the histogram of radioactive decay rates was just as differentiated, that is, unsmooth, as that for the enzyme and chemical reaction rates. Second, the two simultaneous histograms were similar.

He constructed histograms from iron-55 decay data and found that increasing the number of measurements did not smooth out the curve as expected, but in fact did the opposite, making the fine structure of the curve more pronounced. (**Figure 6**)

Shnoll writes: "The nature of the processes we studied in 1978-1985 was so diverse (biochemistry, chemistry, electricity, magnetism, beta- and alpha-radioactivity) that we could conclude: the phenomenon is independent of the type of process." And, "The only common factor for all the various processes we experimented with was their occurrence in the same space-time continuum."

The Shape of Space-Time

Though Shnoll did not find the ultimate random process he was looking for in radioactive decay, he did find a great medium for his study. Radioactive decay, especially alpha decay (the emission of a helium nucleus of two protons and two neutrons), is practically independent of incidental factors. Experimenters have tried since its discovery to change its half-life, its macroscopic rate of decay, by subjecting radioactive samples to extremely high temperatures, pressures, and fields, to no avail.

What Shnoll observed did not contradict the constant nature of a nucleus's half-life. What he did see, however, is that the supposedly random, microscopic changes had a structure, and that structure was akin to that observed in so many other processes. Unlike enzymatic activity or chemical reactions, however, radioactive decay measurements are easily automated, need much less preparation, can be left alone for extended periods of time, and can be measured with high time resolution. Experiments were so easily automated that a portable version of the whole experiment was put on ships sailing to the Arctic and Antarctic, enabling the first synchronous experiments comparing results from widely separated geographical locations. Another important advantage of radioactive decay experiments is that alpha decay has a direction, and therefore spatial effects can be investigated.

By placing radioactivity and chemical experiments on a ship traveling to the Indian Ocean, Shnoll's team found that histograms recorded at Pushchino and near Madagascar—6000 miles away but at nearly the same longitude—were synchronized. Results from radioactivity measurements in Lindau, Germany, however, showed histograms that were similar those at Pushchino, but offset by one hour, exactly corresponding to the difference in longitude between the two places. There seemed to some dependence on local time.

On the other hand, expeditions into the Pacific Ocean revealed another synchronicity that did not depend as much on local time and seemed to observe "absolute time" or a global time: that is, histograms were similar simultaneously, without time zone offset.

FIGURE 7

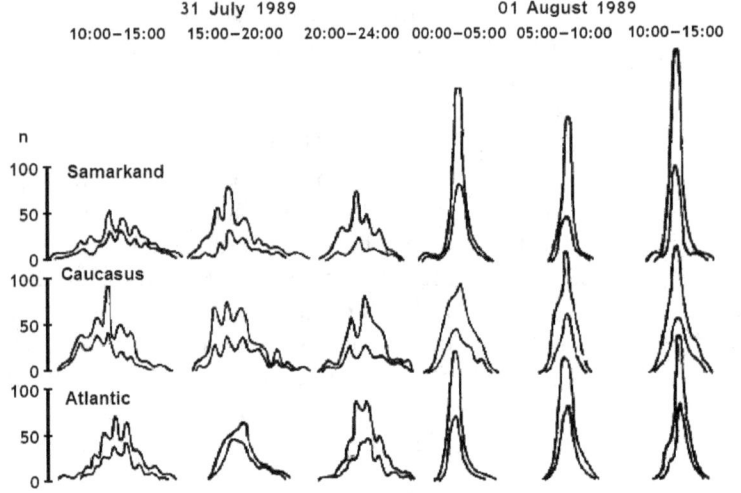

Original Caption: Figure 5-7. Simultaneous changes in histogram shapes constructed from measurements of acetic acid + dichlorophenolindophenol reaction rates at different geographical locations (all around [42° North Latitude]): in Samarkand, in the North Caucasus (the Art. Sernovodsky), and on a ship on the Atlantic Ocean, in the night of July 31 to August 1, 1981.

Figure 7 shows another finding of absolutely synchronous changes in three widely separated locations.

While comparing histograms, Shnoll and his team

FIGURE 8

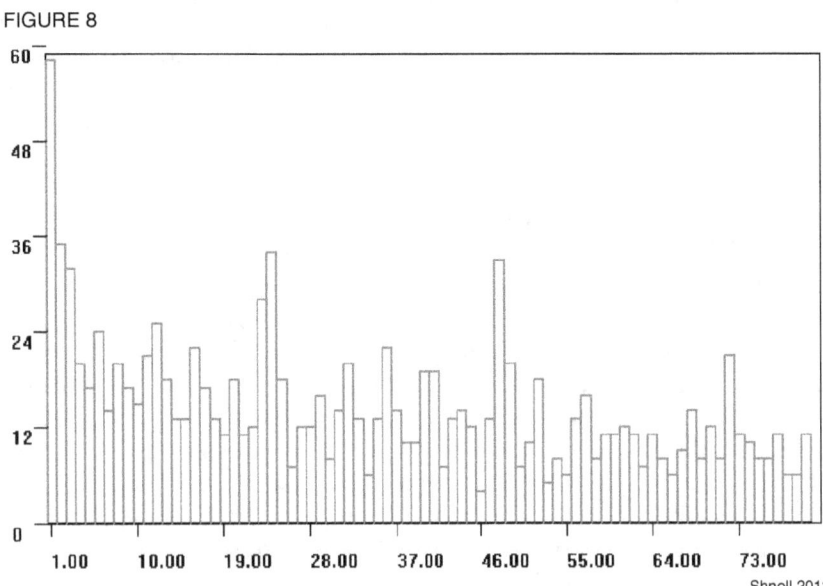

Interval charts like this one disclose the intervals at which histograms are similar. For example, if every histogram were similar to one 24 hours from it, no matter what time it is, then there would only be a bar above 24, 48, and 72 hours. This chart is Figure 5-4 in Shnoll 2012, which shows results of comparison of one-hour histograms constructed from the results of ^{239}Pu alpha-activity measurements on May 18, 1998 in Pushchino.

also noticed that histograms that were one day apart were similar. In other words, a histogram may be unlike another produced from data taken minutes later, yet be strikingly similar to one taken 24 hours later.

From comparing the time intervals at which histograms were similar, they made interval charts, such as **Figure 8.** From these time interval charts, many unexpected relationships were revealed.

Schnoll took up a suggestion that he look for similarities using the sidereal (stellar) day rather than the solar day. They differ by 4 minutes. In solar time, the moment of sunrise tomorrow is determined by a combination of the Earth's rotation on its axis *and* its travel along its orbit around the Sun. But sidereal time is independent of Earth's travel along its solar orbit.

Shnoll refined his histogram intervals to minutes rather than hours, as shown in **Figure 9**, and compared them (he took one-second counts of decay, and made histograms of 60 different counts, amounting to one minute). When he did this, his 24-hour peak clearly separated into two peaks: one at 24 hours (1440 minutes) and one four minutes earlier (1436 minutes), exactly corresponding to the time it takes any particular place on Earth to come back to the same star (or seen inversely, for a star to come back to the same place in the sky).

From these data Shnoll concluded that, "a histogram shape depends on its exposure towards the sphere of fixed stars (or the 'crystal canopy,' as poets used to say). This moved a possible cause of the 'macroscopic fluctuations' beyond the solar system. We got wind of inquisition fires when people inquired about these results."

Why would radioactive decay, seemingly unaffected by many extremes, be concerned about the fixed stars so far away?

Early in his researches, Shnoll had noticed similarities in histograms of reactions of acetic acid and

FIGURE 9

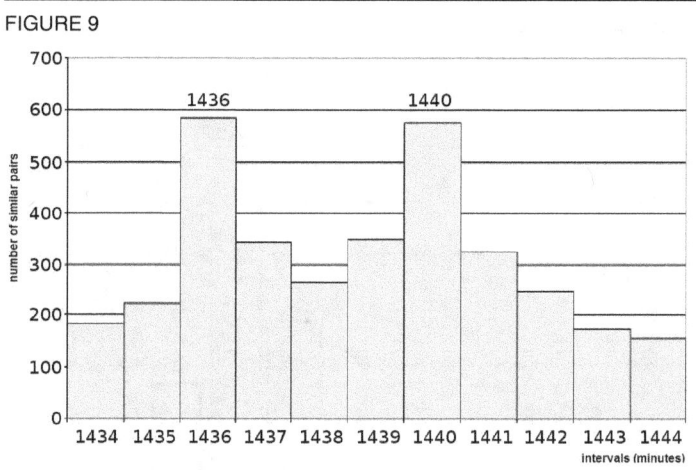

Shnoll 2012

Original caption: Figure 6-4. We observed two separate periods from measurements of ^{239}Pu alpha activity with detectors located in the plane parallel to the plane of the Celestial equator: the first equals one sidereal day (1,436 minutes) and the second equals one solar day (1,440 minutes).

DCPIP one year apart, and had begun taking measurements at the same time every year. He came back to these experiments and performed them more precisely, using plutonium-239 alpha decay. Again he found that the year split into two types of years, as shown in **Figure 10.**

One peak occurred at 365 days (526,600 minutes), when high noon occurred 365 times per year (the calendar or solar year), while another occurred a quarter of a day later (the sidereal year). (We reconcile the two with the addition of a leap day every four years.)

There was even another peak, which was unexpected and completely unexplained. Its period was one minute less than the full calendar year. (**Figure 11**)

Since this cycle could not be explained by cycles within the the Solar System, Shnoll hypothesized that it may be caused by motion of the Solar System with respect to something external to it.

Again, why would decay rates or chemical reactions care about their orientation to fixed stars? Or even the Sun? Also, what would be common to all the different types of processes tested?

As mentioned, alpha decay also has the advantage of being oriented in space. The helium nucleus is not always thrown off in the same direction. In an extensive series of experiments, Shnoll and his team used collimators (directional detectors), to look at the changes in decay rate in various directions—east, west, continu-

ally toward the Sun, and toward Polaris, the star toward which Earth's axis is currently pointing. From these experiments, he was able to reveal a clear anisotropy (non-homogeneity) in space. That is, direction matters. For example, certain astronomical cycles would be revealed in one direction of decay but not another.

This is just a small sampling of thousands of experiments and surprises described in *Cosmophysical Factors in Stochastic Process*. Every experiment was repeated many times to convince Shnoll's most harsh critic, himself. He had to eliminate all possible sources of error. For all other critics, his message was, "Instead of yelling, why don't you just go to the lab and repeat our experiment?"[2]

Read the book!

More Work To Be Done

The work of Simon Shnoll and his collaborators opens up many new domains of research. The few answers they have provided only serve to stir up more questions by orders of magnitude.

First, there are the threads of research Shnoll clearly indicates would be important, but for which he has not had enough hands to continue. These include the experiments with proteins and their "macroscopic conformations." What could these experiments tell us about proteins and life? Or about how the shape of space-time is reflected in other or larger life processes?

Experiments at the north and south poles, testing for effects of the solar day as compared to the sidereal day, and other effects such as the anisotropy of space, remain to be done.

Other avenues more broadly include ways to probe the shape of space-time. What features are shared by every process? Conversely, what features are uniquely expressed?

Several experiments in detecting particular directions of alpha decay prove that directions in space are not equal. Perhaps this anisotropy is due to the motion of the Earth, the Solar System, or even the Galaxy. This could be tested in a manner similar to other experiments

2. This was Shnoll's rejoinder at an "emotional" seminar at the Moscow Institute of Physics and Technology in 1982, where Shnoll first asked for collaborators who would repeat his experiments. *Cosmophysical Factors*, pp. 79-80. The invitation stands: See the Shnoll Lab website at http://shnoll.ptep-online.com/index.html

FIGURE 10

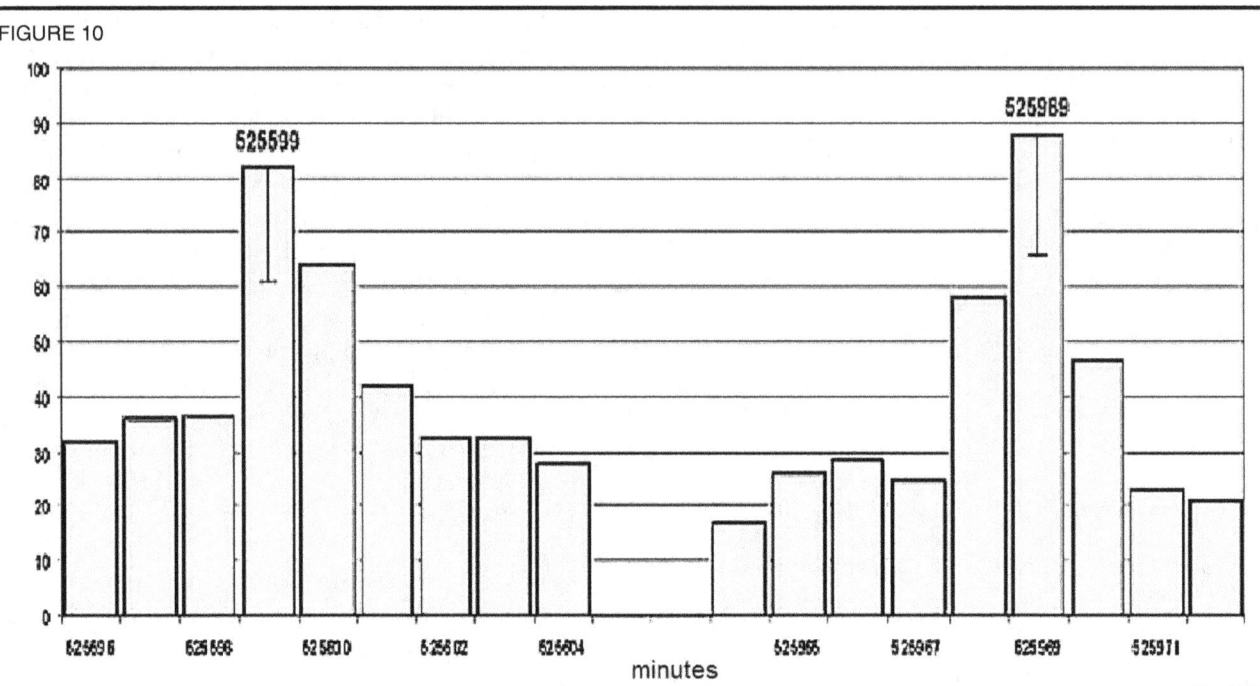

Shnoll 2012

Original Caption: Figure 10-3. Histograms reoccur with a year period that includes two main periods, the calendar, equal to 525,599 and 525,600 minutes, and the sidereal, equal to 525,969 minutes, period; the accuracy of histograms is one minute. Measurements of ^{239}Pu alpha-activity on November 24, 2001 and November 24, 2002.

FIGURE 11

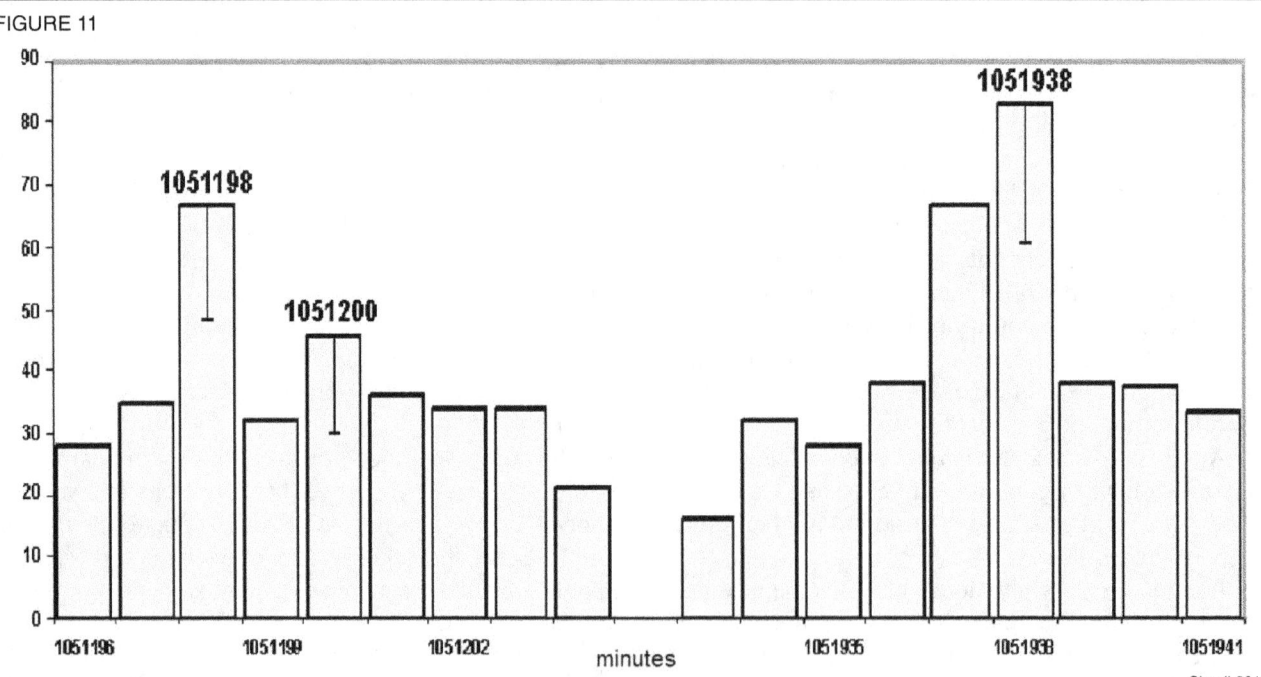

Shnoll 2012

Comparison of histograms over two years shows the sidereal year vs. the solar year (365 days × 2 = 1051200 minutes) drifting by a quarter of a day each year, amounting to half a day over two years, along with another period which lags behind the calendar year by one minute each year, building to two minutes over two years (shown here as 1051198 minutes).

which Shnoll performed involving collimators. Perhaps such experiments will show that anisotropy of space is not due to motion at all.

Perhaps most exciting is a sense of foray into a new physics. Shnoll had a hypothesis that perhaps gravity was at least one of the causes of variation, but experiments during times of high tides produced negative results. Hypotheses of neutrino fluxes as a cause seem to conflict with the definition of the particle as a weakly interacting one. Other hypotheses of concentrations of lepton gases also did not hold. Perhaps the effects of an entirely new, unknown principle are being detected in these experiments in that these factors do *not* influence the histograms, even though the histograms are changing. It may turn out that there is no simple mechanical cause, but only an overall effect of the change of space-time, as Shnoll suggests.

Can these investigations of space-time be used to probe the structure of the nucleus? Perhaps, contrary to a reductionist point of view, the very small is made of the very large.

Vladimir Vernadsky's 1930 discussion of the study of life phenomena and the new physics also resonates here.[3] In this paper, Vernadsky points out two gaping holes in scientific research: (1) universal principles which express themselves most distinctly in life and cognition, and (2) inherent and increasing dissymmetry of living matter.

How does the structure of space-time express itself in cognition? Can we change this structure? Life does exist in the universe. It is not an anomaly. Nor is cognition. In fact, it is these phenomena which may tell us more about the laws of the universe, since they manifest laws unexpressed in the abiotic. Can Shnoll's investigation then be reversed to ask, What then is unique to the space-time of life and of cognition?

Though many questions remain unanswered, one thing is certain—there is no validity in asserting that any terrestrial process is closed, that it can be fully accounted for by terrestrial laws alone.

---

3. Vladimir I. Vernadsky, 1930. *The Study of Life and the New Physics.* Translated by Meghan Rouillard from "l'Etude de la vie et la nouvelle physique," *Revue générale des sciences pures et appliquées*, December 31, 1930. Washington: 21st Century Science Associates, 2015. See http://bit.ly/vernadsky-new-physics

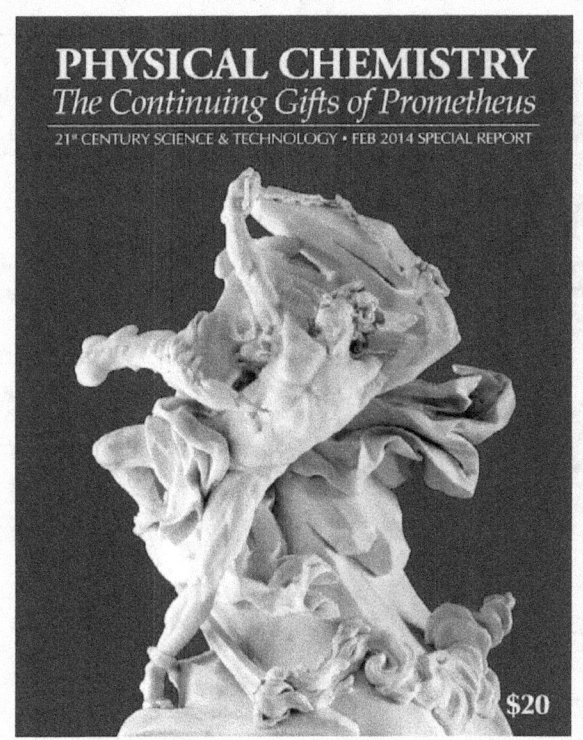

The Mission of Man and How We Pursue It

This is a transcript of excerpts of Lyndon LaRouche's Dialogue with a Manhattan audience on October 10. The dialogue was moderated by Dennis Speed.

Dennis Speed: Okay, we're ready. I'd like to say a couple things today before we start. Some years ago, about 31 years ago, the Schiller Institute put out a book called *The Hitler Book*. It had an introduction I just want to refer to. That book was a contribution to understanding the then-current situation in Germany, and it said, "Its publication has become necessary because processes now at work within the German population are to a large extent unknown to that population, and to such an astounding degree that we must not only draw upon the history of the Twentieth Century, we must proceed from the fact that Germany has never come to terms with its past." Then the book went on to describe the character of Nazism.

The reason I wanted to reference this book, put out at that time by the Schiller Institute, is because this week, we have this spectacle of the erstwhile President of the United States going to Oregon, because of a mass shooting that happens in Oregon, at the same time as the President of the United States *bombs* a hospital in Afghanistan, knowingly and deliberately, without any question. And then, at the end of the week, we have two more shootings, one in Texas and one in Arizona. Yet, people want to ask

The global confrontation personified: President Putin and President Obama meet at the United Nations, Sept. 28, 2015.
kremlin.ru

the question, "What's really going on? We don't understand these processes."

As everyone knows, we have made it our business, day in and day out now for years now, for eight years of the Obama Administration, nearly eight years, to point out that we're dealing with a Satanic personality, and there is an implication for all of us, for every day he stays in office, for how much more dire the circumstances of the United States become.

So we're meeting today, in a particular time, with a very important action having been taken by Russia, but *still* with an action *un*taken in America. And every hour that goes by, we see the consequences of this.

So I just wanted to say that. I hope you don't mind, Lyn. But I was too—you know, this was too much. So, would you like to make opening remarks other than the ones I made? I couldn't stop myself.

Lyndon LaRouche: I've got the picture.

We're in a situation now which is absolutely unique. There's never been a condition like this in terms of the history of the United States, but we have, on the one hand, a very dangerous situation, which is typified by Obama himself, as being the example of relevance. And the other side, we have the questions and answers which we may want to deal with in order to make ourselves happy, in a sense of saying, that if we can deal with this concept of what Obama has represented, if we can understand it,—even though it's an enemy policy,—but if we can understand it, we can then find a solution in our own mind for what the solution might be. And I think that's what's crucial right now.

Speed: Great. Thanks a lot. So, the first question is here.

Cures for New Diseases

Q: It's B— from New Jersey. I get this sense, and I can give a personal note to this, that there's a real change occurring particularly around this flank that Putin has opened up. And I think it's not quite what we saw at the completion when the U.S. astronauts landed on the Moon; but it's more like people getting a sense that "we can do this." You know, not that we did it yet, but that we can do this.

And the personal note I would take on that, is that recently I had a close family member who really has never quite accepted what we've been saying around Obama; in fact, while I was down in Washington, D.C. on Wednesday talking to congressional offices, they called up my household, and even after having just gone through surgery and just starting recovery, they called up not to discuss their own situation, but to discuss with another family member of mine what was going on with Glass-Steagall. And was adamant about that, they did not want to talk about their surgery; they wanted to know what was going on, and had found out that I was down in Washington, talking with congressional offices about this.

So I get this sense that you're seeing—and I've seen this in congressional offices, too; in fact, a meeting I had yesterday, and we were discussing Glass-Steagall and that, and among other things, when I brought up Syria, the staff member said, "Man, Putin is really kicking butt."

So I did just want to put that out there, and see what your thoughts are about this?

LaRouche: No, it's quite appropriate. Putin has actually created a new state of organization in the United States, by doing something which has never been done before. And what he's done has shocked much of the planet, because maybe not some special parts,—but this is really a remarkable operation. And what it means essentially is, that mankind has a higher message to deliver to the rest of humanity. That's exactly what this is, it's a precedent. You know, a lot of things come out of

that. I suppose in most of the discussion other things will come up, that is something we can reference back to, that the fact that there is something which is extremely important, and which, I think, in the course of this dialogue, and so forth today, will come more clearly; by taking parts of what I know about and take each part and then we'll see what happens when we get into that dialogue which is coming next.

Q: My name is L—, and I've worked in health care for many years, not as a nurse, but for an organ procurement organization. Within that context, I was present at the closing of two hospitals in Queens, Mary Immaculate and St. John's Episcopal. I also noted a hospital in Brooklyn, in Brownsville that was a trauma center, and that hospital had been put on the list by the Berger report. But the doctors became very concerned, because they knew the patient population that they serve; so five, high-power doctors within the hospital went up and met with the head of the Health Department, and they promised the Health Department, they said, "give us our hospital back, and we'll make it work!"

I make this comment because there is a severe problem in health care today. Brookdale was able to bring their hospital back online, but that report comes out yearly, and I think this is an example of how our country has deteriorated. And so this was just a comment.

LaRouche: And it was a perfectly relevant comment, because what you're dealing with,—you've got to look at a broader part of the thing, and the detail you represented is actually typical of a larger problem. And that is we don't understand what the meaning of human life is. And when you're talking about health care, you're talking about human life; you're not talking about a disease, you're not talking a particular problem, you're talking about human life. Because the things you will find in health care, go wildly beyond what anyone had known before.

And so therefore, the question is, what is this magic principle, which most people have never fully understood before, at least in the particular examples? What is the thing that makes us enabled to solve that problem of the previously unknown case? In other words like a sickness that comes on, and there was no precedent for that sickness, at least in terms of the practical expression of it. And therefore, the question is, what is our ability as mankind, to investigate, and successfully so, solutions for previously unknown diseases.

youtube

The population at risk: A hospital in the Cincinnati metropolitan area about to be demolished in July of 2015.

Putin's Operation is Unprecedented

And the unknown diseases as just a typical case of the thing; there are other applications of the same thing. Mankind must qualify as mankind, to deal with previously unknown kinds of diseases, and problems as such. And that is something which we've lost, we've lost that kind of ability which was there two generations earlier; you know, I'm an older man, and so I know things like that, two generations earlier.

So that's it. We have to understand that we don't know a fixed solution. We have to have the ability to discover a solution for a problem we had not previously known. And that is, of course, the acme of the practice of medicine.

Q: My name is I—. I've been following fairly closely at least the news coverage of the war against ISIS in Syria and the surrounding area. I guess what's come to concern me, and I wanted your comment on it, was the fair number of reports in the press that the U.S. military or CIA is supplying TOW missiles to the so-called "moderate" jihadists in response to the Russian initiatives. And there's generally a lot of talk of aiming to mire the Russians in Syria the way they were bogged down in Afghanistan in the 1980s.

So my question is, to what extent do you think the United States will actually start intervening non-covertly, to bog down the Russians, in this war with ISIS, and more openly support ISIS?

LaRouche: Against Putin, I don't think Obama or people like him have any case. I think they have no option of that nature. Whereas what Putin has done has never been done before, that kind of operation. Imagine, here are people, take planes; they fly them over unprecedented distances into covert or quasi-secret locations. They do it again and again. It's unprecedented in the recent history of warfare, in conflict.

So Putin has brought into existence, not some miracle statement, but a developed idea, a developed concept of practice, which has done this job. Otherwise, it would have been impossible. If Obama had dominated the area, the whole thing would be a disaster. It's a difficult problem now; they have complications. For example, Germany is part of this whole picture, even though it's not a neighbor of that picture. But that's a problem to handle.

And I'm sure that Putin now has now got a clear understanding of what he's doing; he probably is going to make innovations, because it's his nature to make innovations,—not to just go through a repertoire, but to look at his ability to affect something. And that's what he's done. And it's what Obama has no comprehension of! And most of the leaders in Europe have no comprehension of it. There's some people in China who have a comprehension; there are other people in Asia who have a comprehension, and know what it involves.

But this is something new. It is not an exact model of anything; it is something new which was improvised and developed by Putin's leadership. And that's the way you get it. You have to find solutions for previously unknown diseases, previously unknown problems. And the art of the thing is, where is the leadership which is prepared to adequately deal with unknown conditions, preconditions? And that's what's happened with Putin. He's moved in on something that has never been done before; it has aspects which look like something that has existed before, but it's not.

And therefore, Obama has gone wild. And Obama of course, launched this attack on the hospital and mur-

A grave threat: Obama in the Oval Office, Oct. 5, 2015.

White House/Pete Souza

dered people! Just plain murdered them. He not only did it, but after he was warned that he was doing that, he still continued it!

So this is the kind of problem. The problem now is we've got to change the characteristic of the way in which the United States and other nations, just aren't doing it right. They're failing again and again and again. There are some people in every part of this European area, and elsewhere, who are working in the right direction.

No Deductive Solutions

But the actual solutions are generally unique, of important issues. You start with an understanding of the nature of what you suspect the problem is. But then you find the problem is not quite the thing you thought it was beforehand. And therefore, you have to have the ability to react to that fact, and find a solution quickly. In other words, you start with a probable approach to solve a problem, which is already something good. But in order to defeat the problem, you've got to go a step further, and make discoveries of things that you, yourself, had not even thought of before.

Q: May name is R—, I've been born and raised in Brooklyn all my life, and the greatest change I have seen in all my time is the change of how society thinks. If they thought conservatively, or that I could do it, in our days, and you went out to do something, you just did it. But now, everybody's so ultimately liberal, that somebody vile as Obama got into office, they don't think who's running, assess the politicians that are involved and that's what's getting us in trouble. And all the colleges have all these liberal professors, all these schoolbooks are twisted; they don't give 'em American history to tell 'em what we are. So, how to get people back on the right thinking, I think is a great challenge, and I'm wondering if you have an answer for that.

LaRouche: I think I have a good answer for that. I'm not a perfect person but I happen to know a few things, and I probably know more than a lot of people, because of my experience, and the nature of my experience. What we have which is the problem, is the wrong conception of the meaning of mankind.

Now, mankind is unlike any animal. Mankind has no truly animal characteristics. They say we do, but we don't. I have a nice puppy; she's about four years old, she's a very sweet little puppy, but she's a puppy! She's not a human being; she's not capable of developing human solutions. She will sense doggie solutions; she will mimic what she is capable, as a dog, of doing, and she'll be very happy with the fact that she made the discovery of a new toy or something like that to play with, or a new game to play with.

But mankind is unique. There is no species that we know of which is like mankind. There's no animal that we know of, that corresponds to mankind. But mankind has a value which is often suppressed, by mankind, because mankind operates out of ignorance, largely out of ignorance, and our population in the United States has actually depreciated, degenerated, in respect of my experience in my early life,—that is when I was doing various things back in the 1970s and 1980s and so forth. The kind of things I did then, are things that most people in the United States did not have the experience of. I was privileged in that respect.

But what my point is, is that I understand that you cannot assume that you can make deductive solutions for the future of mankind. Sometimes you'll find something which is useful and which has a deductive character. But the future of mankind depends on a principle.

The point is, what is the nature of mankind? If mankind is unique, what makes mankind unique, relative to all known living processes, including the high ones? What is it? It's the fact of the relationship between the living human being and the deceased human being, those who died or are about to die, because of disease or age or so forth. Mankind is the only species which is actually voluntarily capable, by its own means, in bringing mankind to a higher level of development. No other species can do what mankind is capable of doing, of true creativity, of a type which no animal has. And the importance of mankind, is

U.S. Army/Carmen Burgess
A World War II veteran salutes on the celebration of the 60th anniverary of victory in 2005.

that we as human beings, must in the course of our life, reach the achievement of that, the ability, before you die, that you will have contributed, in your society, somewhere, and given something which mankind had never had before as an opportunity. And therefore, our mission in life is to live a life, if we can, in such a way that we bring mankind to a higher level of mankind's potential as a species.

And that's what's missing. People don't see it. They say, "Oh, people die. So-and-so died." Yes; but what is the consequence of his living or her living, in the process? Especially as the aging process goes on. Does mankind produce a level of development of our species, our society; and can we say, yes, we weep for the death of a valued person. But, what you count on more: did that person make a contribution to the advancement of mankind's ability for the future?

Reach Upward

And that is what the issue is. We lose sight of it, we say that death is the end of mankind. But maybe the person who has died has made a contribution to man-

kind as a whole, for a future. And that is what you're looking at. Einstein, for example, in his time, is an example of that, Albert Einstein. And he was the only person who had an accurate sense of the purpose of human life, as no other scientist of his time had ever achieved. And that's the example that I would hold out; there are other examples of the same nature, but that's a more recent one and a more comprehensible one.

Q: Hi Lyn, this is A—, here again in the city. I wanted to raise with you for discussion the experience that many of us had earlier in the week on Wednesday, in our visit to D.C. It's a trip that I've made numerous times over the past couple of years, though it had been a while. So what was different about it, for me, it was the question that came up in how does this in my mind serve the process of these discussions with you on a weekly basis, oftentimes twice a week, and not just the crisis itself.

So, yes, being down there on numerous occasions was helpful as an experience. And we generally meet with aides or assistants that are younger. And the first thing that occurred to me, was that, why should I approach this any differently than I had in the past, when, really, I'm talking to a young person like I would in any one of our deployments? And that I was going down there with the outlook of being aggressive, not looking to debate, or give a history lesson or a background or a defense; but rather to give a very straightforward account of the crisis as it stands now, and the way out of it, based primarily on your successful record as a forecaster, that is unmatched.

Then, as you would in a street deployment, see how they respond. In some cases, a Wall Street lackey was before us, and before he actually packed up to leave,— always this kind of miracle meeting comes up that he has to leave to. But you know that, and that was fine, because that, too, had an effect; let'em run.

However, there were some young aides there, that had a very different response when you present them with the straight-forwardness of the truth, and now, you're actually in—it's brief, but there's a dialogue; they have questions, they want to know. They're no longer, even for a brief period, a lackey or a Representative, we hope, of that particular Representative's office that we're in. And so, for the first time, I felt I had now the potential to build on a relationship that's useful, within that office, where it might not have existed otherwise. And again, I point to what I think is just the natural process of working through these discussions with you,

EIRNS/Eli Santiago

LaRouche PAC organizers near the United Nations hold a rally on Oct. 5, 2015.

where this comes together. And this time I did not feel like I left anyone's office with my tail between my legs, or feeling like I did not say that which needed to be stated.

So that's in essence what happened, and I think this is true for many of us that went. Obviously, like I was once new to the process, there were those that were new and didn't say much. But I think for most of us that have been doing this for a while, that may be a fair assessment of how we approached it.

LaRouche: There are two aspects to it, what you outlined. Two aspects. One, you have the exposure to people that you can exert some kind of influence on. That is not always, in itself, useful as such. But it may create a doubt, or a concern (as the Quakers would say), in terms of what the experience is that the person or persons you're talking about would consider.

But the other thing, what you're looking for is to reach upward, is to do it as much as you can, reach upward. That is, to try to enlighten the persons you are addressing. It doesn't mean it has to be explicit, it may be just influence. You make a suggestion, and the person may be influenced by that suggestion, not in the sense of a solution, but saying "I've got to add that into my repertoire, and I've got to think about it."

That's what we're looking for. We're looking for the ability to increase the number of people who are responsive to being educated in that sense, being provoked into making discoveries; or not making discoveries, but something's bothering them; they want to solve that problem. They find the problem is challenging, and since they like the idea of that challenge, they want to bite on it for a while. And that is often what we're trying to do. We're trying to create an influence within our society, an influence, and let the good evidence fly wherever it will fly, wherever it can induce an improvement of the outlook of people. And what you have to do is, then, is you have the specialists, who become more qualified in getting at this problem and getting solutions, and that's essential.

Our Divergences Can be Helpful

But you have part of society,—as long as society is responding to the idea of the future, of solving things which constitute the future, either among a group of people, or as something absolutely new. And they are very closely related. Obviously, the most important thing is the discovery of new discoveries, of qualities of mankind's future; like a new invention, a true invention, a new scientific principle, which I have a lot of experience with myself.

So therefore, these kinds of things are kind of a mesh, with people with various degrees of progress, or potential progress, as opposed to people who are not making progress in that way. That's the way you have to look at it. And those who aren't performing, well, you put yourself in favor of the person who is doing something, or is moving in a way to direct something. And you got little less effort on behalf of trying to persuade someone who is not willing to take that route.

Q: Good afternoon, Mr. LaRouche, this is S— from Manhattan, and I want to ask a modified question from last week. I asked what you thought about the President of Argentina asking about calling Barack Obama a traitor to his nation and to the world; in context to Xi Jinping and his hard-line stance on building a New Silk Road and a win-win situation for the entire world. How can we take those two aspects and combine them together and march forward as a political action committee?

LaRouche: They're really both closely related. As a matter of fact, if you put them in the same environment, you wouldn't see the difference; you would see the same kind of convergence, that they would be happy to discuss whatever differences they had, in that context. Because, the thing is, mankind must develop; mankind must acquire the future, the mastery of the future. And as long as people are working for the future of mankind, efficiently doing that, more or less efficiently, or teasing people out of it, or stirring people up, so they begin to catch a new idea they hadn't known before,—that's the way it works. It has to work that way.

What we do in that case, we have a lot of divergence among our own people. But, divergence is not necessarily bad. There may be some people that get it quicker, some people never get it and so forth; but in point of fact mankind *is* reaching out, will find themselves *drawn* into reaching out. Many people don't become inventors by intention, but sometimes they get lessons from history, which come upon them by surprise. So that has to be included.

Q: [follow-up] Also, I just found out something urgent, before I arrived. It got leaked from the TPP that all someone has to do, once the TPP is actually up and going, is make a single complaint about one of your videos on whatever platform it may be, YouTube, Google Talk or whatever, and they have to take your sponsorship on their website down. How do you feel about that? That's a really huge step of censorship and Nazism.

LaRouche: The question is there's a criterion which you're always working with. You're not working with an isolated criterion. You're basing on a general truth, and you have all kinds of truth and non-truth floating around the atmosphere. So what you're concentrating on first is those things which are valid. Now, the question is what degree of validity do they represent. But as long as we're getting progress, and we're not getting resistance to progress, we don't want to complain too much. Because what you want to do is you want to spread the influence, which leads people to converge upon goals which are necessary for mankind. And if you can move people to do a little more thinking, about scientific matters and other matters, that itself is progress. Mankind is not just an isolated brain. Mankind has a manifold capability; human beings have manifold capabilities. And therefore, what we want to do is we want to stimulate those kinds of capabilities, and harvest them, and find a good place to harvest them. And otherwise, we're looking for the progress of mankind, and we assume that the progress of mankind has something to do with the interrelationship within mankind.

Our Job is to Educate

Q: Good afternoon, Mr. LaRouche, I'm I—. The other day I went to Washington with other members of the group. And it was quite astonishing to me to see how some of the office aides were so defensive, in the way in which they were just trying to shield their bosses, I mean the Representatives. But before we left some of the offices, we were able to maybe plant a seed in some of the aides' mind. I have an extensive experience with people working in offices, because this has been my type of work, because I used to teach people how to be office workers.

But I think there is something in Washington which trains those people to be dangerous. I have a way about me. I left a few little seeds as a reminder, to some of them. I told one gentleman that Wall Street is running on the money of drug money, so there is no real money on Wall Street, but drug money. He was like red in the face.

In one of the offices J— and I went and were talking to a gentleman, who said he had a meeting, but he just wanted to avoid us. So, you know, we planted a few seeds in his brain, and I hope he will be able to use that to the advantage, because I let him know Glass-Steagall was implemented in 1933, and Clinton destroyed it in 1999, so he can do the math.

So, I would like to know from you, what would you suggest about these young office workers who are dangerous in Washington, D.C.?

LaRouche: Well, obviously, the reason they're dan-

"The Country School" by Winslow Homer, painted in 1871.

gerous is because they were cultivated to be dangerous. Most of them didn't go into the idea of being dangerous on their own, but they find themselves as subordinates of some people; and then there are some cases who are really outstanding thugs, or something like that. And that's the difference.

So the problem is, how do we deal with this problem? Which means we have to assess the people who are in government, or in similar kinds of positions, like teaching and so forth. And you don't want the bums to influence the schools. You wish to have people progress, and progress along a route of truth; what is actually truth, as mankind may be able to discover truth, where they hadn't know what the discovery was beforehand.

And so therefore that's the issue. The issue is, you have people who are operating on good faith, they may make mistakes, but they're not malicious in terms of their mistakes; they're just doubtful, they just don't know. Well, our job, therefore, is to try to educate them, and to try to exert influence which will educate them. Because it's not always the person who educates the person, it's sometimes the education occurs as a by-product of their experience. And if you find it working that way, just accept that, right away, get to work on it.

Q: Good afternoon, Mr. LaRouche, R— from Brooklyn. On Thursday night we had Jeff [Steinberg] on the Fireside Chat, and we were talking about how we would get rid of Obama, and how we would get the Glass-Steagall Act in, etc. Now, if we did get the Glass-Steagall Act in soon, assuming tomorrow we got rid of Obama, and he was put out under our Constitution, Vice President Biden would be automatically President. Is there any indication that Biden, as President, would be more likely to put the Glass-Steagall Act into effect, sign off on it?

LaRouche: On his own volition, no. He might be induced to do it, but it wouldn't be his intention. He's been corrupted too long and too deeply.

Q: Mr. LaRouche, my name is A—, good afternoon.
LaRouche: Good afternoon, good to see you again.

Q: Always a pleasure to see you. I wonder about the thing about the hospital bombing, is just the top of the long laundry list of all the things Obama's done. He should be removed under the 25th Amendment.
LaRouche: There's no question about that. There's no real question. Think about the history of the Bush and Obama Administration in this succession. What happened to the people in the United States, what happened to them during that tenure of the Bush Administration, the last one, and the Obama Administration? This was absolutely destructive! And the conditions of life inside the United States are really perilous. This is so evil, it's beyond belief. But Obama was the worst.

What Science Really Means

Now, Obama was a more characteristically evil person. And the Bush family,—one Bush was very bad, but the other one was just stupid, and that was the problem. But with Obama, coming into his full flurry, or whatever it is; from the first time, I challenged him early in his first term in office, and he got very angry about what I did, in my reporting of what was wrong with what he was doing, the corruption he'd already embodied at that time. So, that's the way things go.

But the problem is that the destruction that was accomplished under the last Bush Administration, and now the Obama has been one of the most evil kinds of destruction of the people of the United States, the culture of the United States, the most evil thing that's happened so far. And I've known a lot of the history of this nation of ours, and Obama has been the worst of them—absolutely criminal. If you look at the history of Obama's family and look at him as a young boy, and talking about his stepfather there. That this guy was absolutely evil, *absolutely* evil. And Obama has been absolutely evil, in the full record of his Presidency. And that guy should have been thrown out of office before he got in there.

Ziad al-Mehwari

Obama policy: The results of a May 15, 2015 drone strike in Yemen, in which up to 26 civilians died.

Speed: Lyn, this is from somebody who's not here today. He's a former English professor at this institution, CCNY. He's Eric Larson. He wrote a book, *A Nation Gone Blind: A Nation in an Age of Simplification and Deceit*. He was an English professor [LaRouche laughs]—and he watched the drawing and quartering and emulsification of the English language and its usage for 33 years here.

Here's what he said; he couldn't be here today. He lives in the Upper West Side, and he said: "Ever since we met last week, I've been pondering, assessing, fretting, and thinking." He says, "My outrage is immense, my sorrow bottomless, my anger high, but also my nature is timid and my temperament reclusive. I watch and listen but almost never speak unless in very specific situations like teaching a class, where I'm absolutely certain of my position and my relationship to the other." And he says, "All this has to do with why I'm more of a writer than an activist." But what he said at the end, he has this phrase, which I figured you might have something to say about. He says, "That fact or tale is pretty much told in the end of the Nineteenth Century."

So I decided I'd bring this up, first because he's not here, but because he's turning around in his mind the destruction of language usage. He was very surprised to find that a chief mentor of his, Reid Whitmire, as I believe was the man's name, a poet laureate, was a roommate of James Angleton.

LaRouche: [laughs] Oh-ho-ho!

Speed: Yeah. And Eric was very surprised to find the Congress for Cultural Freedom, and the way that actually affected most of the people that taught him. And that was what caused our discussion. So I wanted to just put this in, because I had given him some of the things you've been saying about language, that have been in some of the discussions, so I just wanted to put that in at this point.

LaRouche: Yeah, this is a big subject, if you want to get what you're presenting in that statement of yours just now. That is a very difficult thing to deal with, from the standpoint of method. Because what mankind requires is the acquisition of the power to advance the condition of mankind.

Now the whole history of mankind has been generally flip-flops, and all the other kinds of things that have gone on in the history of mankind. But there is a pattern there nonetheless, which is a pattern of progress. There are periods of great progress, by some people or by even a larger portion of the people. But what happens in this kind of situation, what you are referring to, is actually not progressive. The idea of imposing a kind of pedagogy upon a population can be a very destructive force, and when I think what I know of the Nineteenth Century, which I was not in, except my father and mother were in that area, but I spent most of my life, so far, in the Twentieth Century. And what you just presented I find disturbing, because that's not the way we get progress.

Sometimes you get an accidental contribution to progress, which will be an exceptional case. But I have a different idea of what mankind's future must be, how mankind must shape his future, what science really means. And I'm a devout scientist in that sense. I don't endorse things if I don't have confidence in that as something worth believing, and what you just presented would irritate me greatly, because that's not the way I want to live. I want to live creating the future of mankind. The important thing is creating mankind's future. And the importance of mankind as a species is, it's the only species which is actually able to *create* the future. And all persons who are honorable persons and accomplished will do the same thing. They will provide a solution to the unknown, what had been previously the unknown.

Dana Carsrud

LaRouche PAC Policy Committee member Diane Sare and the New York City Community chorus, at a musical evening on Sept. 26, 2015.

Rising Above Prior Generations

And that's the only thing you can have confidence in: People who can find in some aspect of their life, a contribution to the creative powers of the human mind, but not just the human mind, as such, but the human population. I believe in the importance of man's progress past the point of man's death. And the purpose of society is that mankind must be able to qualify as making a contribution to the intrinsic future of mankind in some degree, in some way. But without progress, without that kind of progress, there is no virtue.

Q: Hi, Lyn, this is S—M— from the New Jersey/ New York operation and I'm wondering if you can help me shed light on the apparent dichotomy between what we're doing politically, in terms of the impeachment of Obama and the taking down of Wall Street, and what we're doing with singing, why we sing.

You have some funny things that happen, when we're in the field organizing, where people will come up. A lot of our signage is geared towards Glass-Steagall, impeaching Obama, and then we invite someone to our chorus, and they give you a funny look. Or, we have people who are coming to the chorus, who may not actually be—you don't know where they stand politically; so you're singing in the chorus with them and you're not sure if you're going to scare them away by saying, "Hey, we've got to get Obama out; he's a bum."

I have some ideas on what we're doing with the chorus, but I'd like it if you could help me clarify that.

LaRouche: No, I think the point is. If you're talking about Classical composition, what we call Classical composition, which includes, in particular, of course, Mozart and others of that type,—that has its own merits; that progress of music has its own merits. And there are earlier developments in the earlier centuries, which are the same thing. Nicholas of Cusa, for example, is an exemplar in this matter. As many people may already know him or know his identity already.

So that's where the thing lies, and the question is, how does mankind rise above a generation which has previously lived? How does mankind make a contribution to the future of mankind, an explicit contribution to the future of mankind, something which mankind has never known before in terms of type? And our objective should be that we insist that we, if we are able, will actually create something which belongs to the future.

Now this happens in families; it happens with all kinds of people,—that people, before they die, may often make a contribution to the future of mankind, a kind of contribution which reverberates into the future. And that is probably the most appropriate prototype for mankind's progress. Can we each make a contribution which is a contribution to the future, to create something which has never been known before, or a factor which has never been known before, which is valid for mankind.

Because when mankind dies, people die. Can they achieve the success of their own development which is a contribution to the future of mankind? And everyone should—the idea of the school system as such and the child developing through successive layers of education and so forth. But progress, in that sense, systemic progress, is I think the measure of what defines mankind as successful. It's the ability to create an influence within society, an influence of principle in society which brings mankind into the area of something which mankind had never known previously. That's the principle of the thing.

Q: Good afternoon, Mr. LaRouche, thank you for taking my question. I was reading a book for some class that I took, and it was Richard Duncan's *The New Depression.* And he spends a lot of time giving all the math for QE1, 2, 3, and so forth, but he doesn't go into any connecting the dots, because of course he'd never get a job again in finance if he did. [LaRouche laughs]

I had a question about the destruction of money through debt, and I was wondering, is that a pathway to a new currency? Since most of what is purported to be wealth is really digital on the books; it's not printed currency or physical. And yet, you see when companies go bankrupt, that have a great value, because they become insolvent with no cash flow, their assets are sold off on pennies for the dollar. And that of course is a part of boom/bust capitalism; it's for the benefit of whoever is holding the cash. Or has enough digital figures in their balance and their check balance to buy up everyone's physical and real assets. So even Stiglitz said something the other day, someone mentioned it to me here from the group, that the Greek debt, it could just be figured out if it was done through electronic payments and reorganized that way.

So my final question, is this digital currency really where it's headed? There was a section in Obamacare, and it's supposed to be implemented in early 2013, that people are supposed to get RFID chips, and then what

Nuclear Energy Institute

Despite well-meaning attempts by various presidents, there has been no net progress in the United States since FDR died. Here, President Eisenhower signals the start of construction of the country's first nuclear power plant at Shippingport, Pa. in 1954.

follows on that, is eventually people would get money through the system. And I noticed this years ago, that all of a sudden, they were just giving out—it wasn't food stamps any more, but they were done through credit cards through Chase! And even in the farmers market in Union Square here, in New York, everyone is having this; it's like one out of six people in the country is on a food subsidy. And Chase makes money on that; even when they interview someone from Chase Bank, he sort of like smiles slyly and says, "yeah, they do very well with that."

So is this where it's all headed: digital currency and the RFID chip?

Shut Down Wall Street

LaRouche: I think the point is, look at Franklin Roosevelt's role in this thing. And you understand, this was never true. This was never a true operation, at all. Because Franklin Roosevelt created a reform, which lasted, first of all as long as he was in service. But also, when he was being booted out of the Presidency, by being squeezed out, along with his companions, there was a destruction of the economy of the United States which followed immediately after Franklin Roosevelt's death. The day that Franklin Roosevelt actually died, was the beginning of the end of the policy of Franklin Roosevelt.

After that, there had been people who tried to do an honest job,—some leading people from the military service of World War II; some other people of the same category; some other people in a later period, who meant to do well. But generally, the problem of the United States has been, that since Franklin Roosevelt died, there has been no net progress in the welfare of mankind in the United States, none! Everything we've gained, if you look at it,—and I've been through the whole thing, especially coming out of World War II,—I tell you, there was nothing ever good, in net effect, even by well-meaning Presidents, because they were either killed, like Kennedy; he was killed, he was murdered! And his brother was murdered, other people were sabotaged. Reagan, was assassinated; he didn't die, but he was assassinated by a Bush, a member of the Bush family. And I was a key person in the service to Reagan. And so, in due course they got rid of me: They threw me in the jug. It was a fraud.

So the point is, the fate of mankind, since that period, since the best period, the Kennedys and Reagan and others who were decent people; but since that time, we've had very little. We had some things from Bill Clinton, in two terms. The first term, he was successful; the second term, they really muscled him out. They let him complete his second term, but they ruined him in the process. It was done by the Republican Party leadership and it was done, also, by order of the Queen of England, who personally did that! Since that time, we've had no good Presidents. And that's reality.

So we have to get back to the point that we actually get a Presidential system, a true U.S. Presidential system, and we have to get it *quickly*. And we have to take some of the actions that Franklin Roosevelt had used in his term of office. We have to shut off Wall Street! Wall Street has to be shut out completely, just shut it down! No payments to them, nothing! They've got nothing coming to them—except pain. And we don't want to have too much pain running around.

But anyway, that's the point. We're dealing with a point where you can't say, this and that period, and this and that period were somehow characteristic. The point was, the process is what's characteristic. And the ups and downs of the development of the process, the ebbs and flows in the process; and most of the stuff in the Twentieth Century has been crap. And Franklin Roosevelt was an exception, and some other people were, who also got killed in due course. So that's the way it is.

Now the point now, is, what're we going to do, to fix that? What're we going to do, to fix what the United States was intended to be? What was it? What is it? And

GDFL/Beyond My Ken

The headquarters for Standard and Poors on Wall Street, ripe for conversion into something useful.

how do we make it work? How do we bring it in and make it work? As an idea of a progress of mankind, a progress of the human species! A progress of mankind!

We all are going to die; all people die. It's what happens in the course of time. *But!* What is the meaning of the life which was lived? And what must you do, to make that life to be lived, as meaningful for the progress of the future of mankind? That's the only way to deal with it.

Q: [About Wall Street.]

LaRouche: Oh, Wall Street. Well, we can put Wall Street— oh, very simple thing: First of all, we have a lot of buildings in Manhattan, tall buildings! Some smaller, some not so pretty, some not so attractive. But we have them. Now what do we want to do with all these dumps, which we call the Wall Street area? Wall Street? Well, what we want to do, we want to get these guys, the Wall Street bunch, throw 'em out. Throw them immediately out, because they're all bankrupt, they're hopelessly bankrupt. They have no merit to them, no value to them. Just dump 'em out.

Now we take those buildings and the skyscraper buildings in the Manhattan area, and the other areas of these types, of some value; and we take 'em over. Who? Not ourselves, no. We say, this is a property of the United States, as a property. So Wall Street sinks. And we let Manhattan take it over, and get a new system of economy. We take over these buildings which are not otherwise usable by human civilization, and we use those buildings now for various kinds of purposes. Some of them, the large skyscrapers have some very useful purposes, very convenient, a very convenient way of simplifying the matter of getting around inside Manhattan; in that alone, among the functions we can supply, by just taking these things over.

But the first thing you must do, is dump Wall Street. Wall Street must be discarded, it must be shut down. It must become nonexistent. And it has to come fast. Because we can't afford Wall Street any more. [laughter]

Germany Can Do It, —But Germany Must Change!

by Rainer Apel

This article, written for Neue Solidarität, *the weekly newspaper of the German Solidarity Civil Rights Movement political party (BüSo), elaborates the ideas expressed in Helga Zepp-LaRouche's* EIR *article in the Oct. 9 issue, "In the Face of the Refugee Crisis: Realizing a Grand Vision."*

Oct. 10—Is the mood shifting? Is the openness shown in the last weeks towards the refugees definitively over, now that it appears that the total will ultimately reach one million, 1.5 million, or more? Has Germany reached the limit of what is possible? Are federal, state, and local authorities no longer able to handle it? Must the budget be cut somewhere else to pay the costs of the refugees, as Finance Minister Wolfgang Schäuble and other adherents of the "zero deficit" dogma claim?

Finally: Must a new city as large as Munich be conjured from the ground every year to provide decent accommodation for all of the refugees?

Poor Germany! How far have you sunk, if everything the opinion-making mass media puts out these days is true! How, then—one must ask—did the Germans manage, both in the East and the West, to accommodate and integrate something like 14 million refugees (!) 70 years ago, shortly before the end of World War II and in the immediate postwar period, refugees from the lost East and the Sudetenland? How were the Germans able to rebuild their bombed out cities so quickly?

In the period before and after 1989, how was it possible for West Germany, once again, to take in another three million refugees from East Germany? And then the 750,000 refugees from the Balkan wars in the 1990s, who were also taken in!

How Germany Did It

Germany was able to do it because it had, at that time—and until the introduction of the Euro at the turn of the millennium—a different economic and financial policy, and indeed, into the 1970s, a *completely* different policy. Financial speculation was at best a marginal phenomenon, and the banking system and financial policy served primarily to promote the real economy and productive jobs, and the creation of real values and real growth.

The postwar, government-owned reconstruction bank (Kreditanstalt für Wiederaufbau), for example, had a policy of promoting the small and middle-sized entrepreneurs (Mittelstand) through long-term, low-interest loans, at least into the early 1970s, a policy applied with great success by the Roosevelt-era Reconstruction Finance Corporation in the 1930s. The

Bundesarchiv

Some of the more than 14 million refugees from the East, who entered and were assimilated into Germany in the last days of World War II and the immediate postwar period. This photo was taken in Danzig (the still-German occupied city of Gdansk, Poland) in February 1945.

German "Economic Miracle" was no miracle: It was the result of a wise, long-range policy in the service of the population, a policy that Germany must urgently return to.

Another constructive example: After the disastrous flooding of the River Elbe in 2002, with losses into the billions of euros, Chancellor Gerhard Schröder ordered the suspension of the EU-imposed budget constraints. He ordered that otherwise blocked funds, necessary for rebuilding the flooded regions, be made immediately available. The infamous "zero deficit" policy was not around then, but unfortunately not for long. And it should be eliminated today, definitively, as part of a whole new approach.

cc/Rebecca Harms

Syrian refguees on their way to Germany, crowding the Budapest, Hungary Keleti railway station, Sept. 4, 2015.

Only in this way will Germany be able to to build new housing every year on the scale of a big city like Munich, and to repair and modernize the nation's roads, bridges, railways, school buildings, and other infrastructure, which was all decrepit long before the great wave of refugees arrived.

Rebuilding the Nation

Well-maintained infrastructure and good housing attract businesses and high-paying jobs, so the municipalities can regain financial strength through increased tax revenues, and 82 million German citizens, plus 1.5 million or more refugees, can make a living suited to the Twenty-First Century. It is not just the New Silk Road that must be built. In Germany also, there is an enormous amount to be done, and that would be the case even if there were not a single Syrian refugee!

The costs of providing for the refugees and accommodating them is only apparently high—but strictly speaking, only a small part of what Germany must invest anyway. The purely domestic investment backlog in Germany is at least several hundred billion euros, and probably quite a few more billion.

As for the expenditures for the refugees themselves, the figures given in the *Bildzeitung* daily on Oct. 6 can certainly be revised upwards: Construction of up to 400,000 new homes per year; up to 25,000 additional teachers; 1,000 renovated or completely new schools; room for 68,000 more children in daycare centers, 10,000 more hospital beds, 6,000 more doctors. Add to that 20,000 new administrative staff positions, 50,000 new social workers, and 15,000 new police officers.

If it is possible to have skilled refugees participate directly in creating a good deal of the needed new capacity and jobs, then the integration process will be largely accomplished. Nothing is more helpful for the refugees in quickly overcoming the suffering and trauma of their journey than actively participating in something productive, which allows them to progress. That is what we experienced in Germany in the post-war reconstruction period .

A negative example is the failure to reconstruct the Balkans after the wars of the 1990s, which left especially young people in Kosovo 80% unemployed, and deprived them of any prospect of improvement. That is what drives them to Germany in the hope they will be better off there.

If we implement the fundamental change in policy outlined above, there will be enough money left to rebuild the cities of Syria, Iraq, and Lebanon, which today look like the cities of Germany in 1945. It will be money well spent; since these and many other countries in ten or twenty years will be counted among Germany's best trade partners, because the German reconstruction aid granted today will not be forgotten.

Every Day Counts In Today's Showdown To Save Civilization

That's why you need EIR's **Daily Alert Service**, a strategic overview compiled with the input of Lyndon LaRouche, and delivered to your email 5 days a week.

For example: On Sept. 30 EIR's Daily Alert featured Lyndon LaRouche's warning that the action must be taken immediately to remove President Obama in order to not only avoid further provocations toward World War III, but to avoid a disorderly collapse of Wall Street.

"If Wall Street collapses in a debt panic, that chaotic destructive force can lead to death and destruction in the United States and around the world," he said. FDR's Glass-Steagall is needed now.

Russian President Vladimir Putin's recent initiative in Syria has weakened Obama and created the necessary opening to do what's needed. But time is of the essence.

This is intelligence you need to act on, if we are going to survive as a nation and a species. Can you really afford to be without it?

THURSDAY, OCTOBER 1, 2015

EIR Daily Alert Service

EIR DAILY ALERT SERVICE P.O. BOX 17390, WASHINGTON, DC 20041-0390

- LaRouche: Wall Street Must Be Shut Down Before It Crashes
- Kerry Confirms Shift in U.S. Policy on Syria, Assad
- Putin Orders First Air Strikes Against Syrian Jihadists
- Russia's Upper House Approves Use of Armed Forces Abroad
- German Government Rejects Turkish Proposal for 'Safe Zones' in Syria
- Senator Warren: Glass-Steagall 'Is Exactly What We Should Do'
- German Saving Banks Threatened by Zero Rates Policy and EU Over-Regulation
- Senator Feinstein Thinks Russia's Move in Syria May Be Positive
- Dana Rohrabacher, Chair, House Subcommittee on Europe, Eurasia, and Emerging Threats, Holds Hearing on Terrorist Threat in Russia
- Rep. Dana Rohrabacher Attacks U.S. Support of Saudis, and Campaign To Overthrow Assad in House Foreign Affairs Committee
- BRICS Foreign Ministers Meet in New York
- NASA May Join Chinese/European Space Science Mission
- Finding Water on Mars Provokes Broad Debate in China
- Secretary John Kerry Reviews the 2013 Powerful Example of Cooperating with

---

✂

SUBSCRIBE (e-mail address must be provided.)

EIR DAILY ALERT SERVICE

- ☐ **$100** one month (introductory)
- ☐ **$600** six months
- ☐ **$1,200** one year (includes EIR Online)

Name _____

Company _____

Address _____

City _____ State _____ Zip _____ Country _____

Phone (_____) _____

E-mail _____

I enclose $ _____ check or money order

Make checks payable to
EIR News Service Inc.
P.O. Box 17390, Washington, D.C. 20041-0390

Please charge my   ☐ MasterCard ☐ Visa
                   ☐ Discover   ☐ Am Ex

Card Number _____

Signature _____

Expiration Date _____

EIR can be reached at:
www.larouchepub.com/eiw
e-mail: **fulfillment@larouchepub.com**
Call **1-800-278-3135** (toll-free)